the

butterfly groove

the
butterfly groove

*A Mother's Mystery,
A Daughter's Journey*

JESSICA BARRACO

SWP

SHE WRITES PRESS

Published 2015
Printed in the United States of America
ISBN: 978-1-63152-800-2
Library of Congress Control Number: 2015936325

Book Design by Stacey Aaronson

For information, address:
She Writes Press
1563 Solano Ave #546
Berkeley, CA 94707

She Writes Press is a division of SparkPoint Studio, LLC.

Dedicated to Dianne Barraco,
for a mother's work is truly never done.

Author's Note

In some places, I've changed the names, identities, and other specifics of individuals who have played a role in my and my mother's lives in order to protect their privacy and integrity. The conversations I recreate in the chapters marked "Jessica" come from my clear recollections of them, though they are not written to represent word-for-word transcripts. Instead, I've retold them in a way that evokes the feeling and meaning of what was said, in keeping with the true essence, mood, and spirit of the exchanges. The action and dialogue I have imagined in the chapters marked "Dianne" come from my research and interviews. The conversations in those chapters are also not intended to be verbatim, but instead were created in my good-faith attempt to relay the exchanges my mother had with the people in her life who meant the most to her at the time.

I squint my eyes over the horizon and watch the tide grow higher as I wring out my doll-size, floral, one-piece bathing suit. It is almost time. "Come on, Jess," my mother yells. "The shakes are on their way." I throw on my pink cover-up and run to her. Behind us, my sister lies asleep on a white beach towel spread out on the sand. My mother and I laugh as the white foam of the water wakes my sister up; looking confused, she goes back to sleep again and continues the cycle. We scream in suspense as the waves rise to their highest peak and breathe elongated sighs of relief as they crash around us without sucking us back into the unknown blue abyss.

When I was a little girl, my mother taught me never to fear an unpredictable tide. Problems, like waves, rise calmly and steadily, with enough time to think in between, she would tell me. You can see problems like looming sets out in the bay. I should not fear the rough, unstable riptides of the Pacific Ocean, or those in my life—my mother had taught me their secrets. I knew their game at the unripe age of five.

I have experienced rough tides—we all have—but then, on that gorgeous late afternoon, everything was at bay. My mother was next to me, and it didn't matter how high the tide rose—she could handle it. It was just us, two plastic beach chairs, and one cookies 'n cream milk shake split clumsily between two cups.

My mother taught me never to turn my back on the ocean. She said knowing how to swim was half the battle, that I had to learn how to manage the strong currents before I could dive in. "If you face the ocean dead-on, there are no surprises. Don't let it sneak up on you—it has a mind of its own." I nodded, lightly shaking salt water out of my eyes and eyebrows, a scratching sensation gnawing at every pore. "Never turn your back on the waves, Sheynah Meydeleh."

At the time, I did not realize just how palpable that statement would be. You always have a choice in life: let the waves crash behind you, or face them dead-on. Let your problems flood your life, or methodically swim through the waves, conquering them one at a time.

I walk down the stairs, fuming with anger. My brows are furrowed to form a line down the bridge of my nose. This always happens when I'm both angry and sad. *Someday, I'll be able to tell my children how excruciating each wrinkle-worthy moment was,* I think. I nearly trip down the second-to-last step as a disgruntled neighbor passes me. I am twenty-three years old and not on my side of town. It took me almost as long to get to Larchmont from West Los Angeles as it would a person to commute from Manhattan to New Jersey. I scuff my Havaianas flip-flops on the cement and look back up at the apartment. She's waving goodbye to me. Kim Kamilla, the first psychic I ever went to see, screams, "Leave fear behind."

I've been going to her for a few years every now and again for tarot card readings. Some people may find this insane; sometimes I think it is. But if people are going to believe in intangible ideas like fate, peace, and love, why can't I believe someone might be able to tell me a few things about my future by harnessing her gift of intuition? She certainly doesn't know all, but she knows something, and for a girl with a turbulent childhood, knowing something is always better than nothing. I grab the cast-iron gate to head out, feigning my last happy wave, and remember the first time I walked up her steps.

I was so nervous then. I was twenty years old and more petrified about life than I would have admitted to you at that time. I think I was wearing a bold T-Bags-branded, studded T-shirt dress that I had purchased on Robertson during one of my "it's okay my college relationship was a failure" shopping sprees. Shopping is one of my favorite hobbies, because, well, the future is imminent; it's totally predictable. You walk into a store, you try on some clothes, you probably buy a few items. Twenty minutes later, you have a new piece to add to your wardrobe that can't talk back or break up with you or change its mind about living in your closet. You are in control. You decide to stop wearing it, give it to Goodwill or throw it out completely. Clothes can symbolize events that live on in the threads forever.

Before my initial visit with Kim, I had thrown away one of the green dresses I wore to the Valentine's Day dinner that resulted in said college breakup the year before. Throwing that dress down the garbage chute was one of the most satisfying things I have ever done. The only regrettable part was not being able to witness it burning in the incinerator. I once fell in love in that dress. I was happy in that dress. Then, eventually, my heart broke in that dress. I felt like a fool in that dress. I suddenly didn't trust the future in that dress.

And that's exactly what I said to Kim the first time I visited her. "You're so young. You shouldn't have a care in the world—why are you here today?" she asked blandly, in a tone I suspected she might use with all of her first-time clients. I stared down at one bejeweled button on my dress for a few seconds, looked up at her, and said flatly, "I'm here because I don't trust the future." Kim smiled and was silent for a few long seconds. She said, "That's one of the best answers I've ever heard." In my head, I felt as pathetic as that statement sounded to me, but it also rang true. I *don't* trust the future. Why should I?

She began to deal the cards, wiping some sweat from her brow. She lived in a sweltering, un-air-conditioned apartment. Outside, I heard some kids playing in the street. I thought of how I never played in the street. "Cut the deck in two when you're done shuffling," Kim said, taking a sip of water. I shuffled the turquoise and jade cards diligently. My mom taught me how to shuffle, but she could make a bridge mid-shuffle, something I was never able to master. One time I almost had the technique down when I was drunk on vacation—but then, once I was sober, I lost it. I thought of my mother every time I shuffled, every time I could not make a bridge. It was one more thing to add to the laundry list of things she was supposed to teach me. I handed the cards over to Kim, and she spread them out. I thought of my mother's eyes. They were a deep, sparkly jade.

"Here is your family over here. I see that your parents are not together. They are very far away from each other." I nodded; well, she *was* a psychic. "Your mother is dead . . ." Her voice trailed off.

"And my father's still here," I said, finishing her sentence. The typical uncomfortable silence followed that I'd grown accustomed to when people realized my mom had passed, and when they deduced that I was probably young when it happened, as was she, set in. So much of my life had been tied up in other people's speechless moments. I always told them, *It's okay; I'm okay.* I always tried to reassure them, when that moment had passed, that I had fully gripped the reality that I was motherless. Apparently, I was a good liar. People bought it every time. Sometimes I did, too.

I've come a long way since that hot summer day in Kim's airless apartment in 2008. I graduated college, got published in national newspapers and magazines, made friends, became an aunt two more times over, and endured another earth-shattering breakup. I realize this while opening the door to my blue Passat, feeling the LA heat radiating through the gray leather seats. I rest my head against the steering wheel as hot tears form in my eyes, but they're not nearly as scorching as the pain in my heart. My skin has it easy. I close my eyes and replay in my head what just happened.

Kim channeled my mother for the first time. I could not believe what was happening, and maybe I still don't. Kim's ability to guide me through the fluff in life—dating, jobs, general instability—seems easier than channeling my dead mother. I respect Kim, and I believe that my mom's spirit lives on, but being able to connect to her seems crazy to me, even though I feel her spirit all the time. I guess this was another part of my intuition I wasn't trusting. I look back at the apartment from the window of my car and see it all again. My mom's spirit was in the room. And she was talking to Kim.

"Your mom is telling me she loved to dance, that you two had that in common," Kim said. I nodded skeptically. I thought, *Dancing. That's an easy assumption—we're women.* "She's showing me she once burned your forehead with a curling iron before your dance recital—you were so mad," she said, smiling. In my throat grew a lump that no amount of swallowing could conquer. I might have choked. I saw the headline in my head: "Girl Dies in Psychic Reading." *This is insane*, I thought. "Your mom says there's a jewelry box you will gain possession of soon. You loved to play with it when you were little."

"The one with the mahogany drawers and gold handles!" I screamed gleefully, almost in a cheerleader's tone, perked up as if my team had just scored a touchdown.

"I think so," she said. "Also, your mom wants you to find these pictures of her from when she was a little girl and include them in your book."

I was mortified. Why was she torturing me? I started out sternly: "Kim, I have no pictures of my mother, or a jewelry box, for that matter. Everything is gone. Somebody, got rid of them, and I gave up looking."

"You don't have to look for them—they will find you."

Oh, please, I thought. I'd worked so hard for everything in my life; nothing had just "found" me. I was torn—I wanted to believe, but how could I? My mother had never seen those pictures.

"There's a picture of your mom, and she's telling me she is about three years old, and she's looking to the side, wearing a blue-and-white party dress, with a bow in her hair. She specifically needs you to find that one." She then stood up, acting out a hypothetical pose my mom might or might not have been in somewhere in 1953—practically a parallel universe at this point.

"Is it in color?" I asked doubtfully, squinting.

"Yes."

I thought, *How could it be in color? It was taken in 1953. Many movies weren't even in color then, much less my mother's home photographs.*

We discussed other things. My upcoming move to New York City. My lack of a love life. How she still thought I would successfully write at least three books. *Another parallel universe,* I thought, *in which I became a published author.*

"You need to find Frank Parker," said Kim. I did not have to ask if my mom had told her that or not; Frank either wanted to stay lost or wanted to be found. And none of us—spirit or human—in the room could know that yet.

I have ambition and drive in my soul, but when things do actually come to fruition, it's nearly unbelievable to me that they'll turn out all right. I probably would have had a stroke if I were Cinderella. The clock would have struck midnight and I would have had paralysis in my face, so that by the time Prince Charming searched the town for me, I would have been on life support, suffering from a droopy face and unable to try on the famous glass slipper. He'd wonder who the nutcase was and move on. *Nice hair, but this girl is crazy yet slightly familiar,* he'd think, and walk right on by.

I start the engine to drive home. *Home:* I use the term loosely. Home was an apartment I moved to and from every year.

I wouldn't be able to hold Kim accountable for uncovering my mother's wishes for several months, but what happened that day did affect me. I felt the glimmer of hope creep back into my heart, like an old friend with whom you've lost touch, and it challenged me to think, *Maybe I can trust the future.* Maybe I could trust it through my mother and her mysterious past.

I was four years old when my mother pulled me into her walk-in closet to show me memories from her past, memories that she kept carefully tucked away. It was her birthday, or maybe the day before, and she was searching for something deep in her closet. I sat down, cross-legged, in my hot-pink dress and looked intently as my mother blinked her large, jade-colored eyes to find the right hiding place. "Aha! There we go," she exclaimed.

Behind her white-plated shoe racks and '80s-inspired black and red pumps lay a pink pillowcase securing a wooden, light brown box. As she pulled it out, she knocked some dust off the top with one quick blow—*wooo*—and opened a small drawer, the interior of which was barely big enough for one of my toy trolls or Polly Pockets to live in. There she found a small note and a picture of a man standing by himself in front of a red-roofed apartment building. I couldn't read yet, so I couldn't make out what the note said. But to my young eyes, I thought the man looked like Sonny Bono. He had a long, handlebar-type mustache and boyish brown hair that I could tell he probably tossed to the side a few times when he was trying to keep his cool. In his eyes I saw something I had never seen before.

"You see this man, baby girl?" I blinked my innocent brown eyes. "He was my ballroom dance partner."

"Is that Daddy?" I asked.

"No, it's not. It's one of my old boyfriends, but he was special, very special," she said in a private tone.

For a second, I could have sworn the twinkle in my mother's eyes mirrored the man's exact expression in the picture—she must have taken it. I felt a sense of magical nostalgia in the air, as if music should have been playing. The imaginary string quartet began.

"This is Frank Parker, someone I loved very much." My mother quickly put the note and picture back in their hiding place, looking almost unsure about why she'd gotten them out to begin with, carefully set the box far behind her shoe rack, and said to me, "Please don't ever go in here by yourself—only with Mommy."

I nodded, and before I could ask a question, she said, "What would you like for a snack? A Push Pop, perhaps?" A distraction tactic—I could not resist those delectable Flintstones Popsicles. As much as I wanted to know more, I could not pass up a Push Pop opportunity. Yet I had learned that there was a man out there whom my mother loved. He was not my father. I like to believe it was at this moment that I became a hopeful romantic.

Every time after that when I thought about that moment, I had trouble sleeping. A few years later, I was wide-awake at midnight, which was late for an eight-year-old. My mind was turning faster than I was able to pedal my Barbie tricycle. I could not relax. Would I be the first eight-year-old insomniac to walk the streets of Orange County? Would I learn the "Thriller" dance while I was at it?

My parents had turned our three-car-garage space into a room for all of my Barbies. Inside this room, on Barbie Lane, as I called it, everything was perfect. No one had cancer and no one was dying. Kens were monogamists, even though there were only three of them, and there were big Barbie families; the smallest one had three children. The families took turns living in the neon-pink dream house. They took turns being doctors, lawyers, and models. They took turns loving each other. I always dreamed of interchangeable relationships, family units that would love each other no matter what.

Skipper, the one who had a little button on the small of her plastic back, knew how to say only two phrases on voice commands: "Let's go to the beach with Ken and Barbie on the weekend," and "Let's go to the mall with Barbie on the weekend." Everything was "on the weekend" for Skipper. Maybe Skipper was a Valley girl masked as Barbie. Perhaps she was just stupid. Skipper may have been a slut in other playrooms, but not on my watch.

There was Vicki, the beautiful brunette, and Doctor Barbie, who wore short white skirts with matching lab coats. She was a freak in the bed and had four children. There was Jade, who was an older Barbie, of my sister's era, so she'd seen a lot—like Debbie Gibson and New Kids on the Block. I always liked Jade, who in hindsight was more like *Les Misérables* Barbie. She was not a looker, and I could never wipe the grim expression off her plastic face. I always wanted to write to

Mattel and ask them how they successfully got dirt on her face. I learned at a young age to pick my battles, however.

There was Chelsea, who was a hairstylist and quite promiscuous, from what I remember. And then there was Kyle (one of the Kens), who had great hair but got sent off to war in 1993. It took me six weeks and two cleaning ladies to get him out of Kosovo, also known as the area behind the random twin bed on Barbie Lane. Vicki was so glad to have her husband home. Of course, his thigh was hanging out of his skeletal body, a battle wound, but she had to wait only until 6:00 p.m., when my dad came back from work, opened the garage door, and said, "I'm home," and I rushed out of Barbie Lane, through the laundry room, and into the hallway. "Daddy, help Kyle—his leg is broken."

Even at six, I realized my parents did not get that these Barbies were my family. They were not just Barbie and Ken; they were Kyle, Vickie, Suzanna, and Kelly. They kept me company when I was alone. They kept me safe my entire childhood. But I didn't expect my family to understand this, so I referred to them as Barbie and Ken in their presence. When I was young, I tried to mask my pain around my family; I internalized it for them. I always knew my place: little Jess. Little Jess was always scared, crying, fearful. So the times when I could internalize my emotions, like on Barbie Lane, I thought I should let my family believe that Barbie and Ken were just toys to me—I was fine, like the other kids. But I wasn't.

Barbie Lane was my Mecca, my saving grace, the love of my childhood. It was the worst when I got sick and my mom would say, "You cannot play in the Barbie Room today because of your sinuses. I don't want you bending over." Then, when she would do her breathing treatments, I would disappear, and no one ever really worried. If you couldn't find little Jessica, you knew where she was—safe and sound on Barbie Lane. Each night I said goodnight to the Barbies, and each morning I said hello. My first thought, the few times in Southern California when I could hear thunder, was that I needed to run downstairs and make sure Barbie Lane was safe in the storm.

No one seemed to notice or, if they did, seemed to care. Barbie Lane was where I learned to be independent, entertain myself, and fantasize about what could be in my future. There was always kissing, there was always nudity, and there was always love. I sound like a flower child; I'm really not. I was a curious child. I yearned for experience. I yearned for perfection. A life without oxygen tubes in my mother's nose, and a life without that hideous trachea implant through which my father had to suction phlegm out of her lungs. A beautiful life without sterilized hospital rooms, and a life where paramedics did not come to my home more often than my uncle from Santa Barbara.

I dreamed of a life without worry and pain, a life where I didn't worry about my mom dying every day. I remember looking out of the backseat window, sitting in a booster seat, hearing my favorite Rod Stewart song. The one that made me cry: "Forever Young." I still cry when I hear it. I used to cry because I would stare out the window of our silver Volvo station wagon and wonder if Rod Stewart would still sing this song if my mom died. Where would she go? Would she be a star, or a blade of freshly cut grass, or a warm blanket over my shoulders on the couch? Now the song makes me cry for different reasons: it makes me wonder if I ever felt young one day in my life. Did I ever feel my age? Now? Then? On Barbie Lane? I feel like I was born twenty-five and have aged accordingly since, which would make me about forty-nine. I don't want to be forty-nine—that's how old my mother was when she died, when she turned into a star, a blade of grass, a Rod Stewart song. Did she ever feel young? All these questions depraved my young mind, like a disease filtering through my pores and into an open wound that would never scab over. So I would count down the hours, minutes, days until I could go into my Barbie room and rejoice in my happy family—even though they were made of plastic. Barbie couldn't save my mother's life, but she certainly saved mine. All sixty-eight dolls saved me.

My childhood made me feel like I always had gum stuck in my hair. I could see the gum, and I could feel it, but no matter how many times I cut it with a pair of scissors, it reappeared again, as if some demon kept blowing bubbles in it. So I learned to chew gum at a young age, to contain my bubbles, to restrain my anxiety about the pinkness getting into my fine, light brown strands. I learned to create fantasies that pulled me out of my reality. I learned that home would eventually be where I was, but for now, it was on Barbie Lane.

No one could touch me there. And people hardly kept me company in there—they would have gotten lost in the mess of Chiclet-size purple pumps, sharp accessories, and shiny, metallic Barbie garments. Whenever my family entered the Barbie room, it seemed as though they thought it was an unhealthy way for me to spend my time, that I was a loner who would always have difficulty making friends. That was never the case. Kids always talked to me; I just didn't like them. I liked only my kindergarten boyfriend, because he was the first frog I ever kissed. The funny thing about fairy tales is that the princess always thinks she's kissing a prince, but, more often than not, it's a toad. Barbie and I would reflect on this more than a few times over the years. Then there came a day when I had to ponder love without her—without all of them. What a shitty day that was.

JESSICA

Spring 2010

*T*he season changed again, oddly, without my mother there. The oddest part of all was that it had been nearly eleven years since she had passed and spring still felt strange without her. I hated seeing the jacaranda trees bloom. It didn't seem fair that they still bloomed without her being alive.

As a little girl, I would watch my mom get ready for the day, brushing her short curls carefully with a blue-toothed comb, putting on straight swoops of mascara seamlessly to highlight the emerald keys to her soul. *Be careful what you wish for*, she would say. I like to picture Fred Astaire or Cary Grant uttering this phrase in an old movie, where a small chirp of a stereophonic studio track would accompany the twinkle in their eyes. I used to sit on my pink-and-purple floral-print bedspread and twirl my sunny brown hair while humming "I'm in Heaven," wishing Fred and Ginger were there to teach me the choreography. *I want a ball gown*, I thought. *I want to twirl in it. I want experience*—moments that didn't linger with feelings of heartache and stomach drops as if I had just gone down the final incline of a wooden roller coaster devoid of a harness.

My childhood was like a theme park with rides that had rusty hinges, broken seat belts, and cold thoughts. Rides I had absolutely no interest in riding. I liked to believe that I was a trouper, until finally, in high school, I realized some profound things. *Who cares that I'm a trouper? I want to live. I want experience. I want the simple life. I want to kiss maybe ten boys, have sex with five of them, and marry one of them. I would like to have three, maybe four kids with that one man and hopefully find a career that I could be good at long past the maternity ward.* It wasn't wrong of me to wish for experience. It was wrong of me not to stipulate that I would prefer my outlying negative "experiences" to stop at twenty-two. Curiosity killed the cat. I don't even like cats. I asked for experience, and experience is what I got. I just wish I had included a simplicity clause in my experience contract.

Maybe today, I think, as I stumble across my mother's old phone book from the early 1990s. The phone book was incredibly important to her. I suppose this happens after years of being a bookkeeper, both professionally and personally—my mom had the only key to all of her treasures, and she wanted to keep it that way. When her life was exposed, she was judged and ridiculed and misunderstood by so many, especially her family. So she learned to keep everything a secret, even her phone numbers. She harbored that phone book the way a cheating man would hide his little black book.

I take a sip of my morning coffee and see it in my mother's sophisticated, cursive writing, in plain view: Frank—followed by an area code and seven digits. I think I'm imagining it at first. How can it just be right there, plain as day? The man I have been seeking for years is right there, in my mother's phone book. Were it ten years earlier, I likely could pick up the phone and call him. His number is written in my mother's hand-writing, which itself is startling since I have barely seen it in twelve years. Of course, it *is* her telephone book I'm poring through.

"Oh my god," I say to myself, setting the mug down on the coffee table, suddenly unable to hold it without shaking the brown liquid out. "I'll be damned." I get my computer out and start typing. Maybe I'll find him today. Maybe I'll finally put the puzzle together. I now know one more morsel of information: my mother and Frank were still talking well into the 1990s. She died in 1999.

As I obsessively Google his name and the number and get ready to call my private investigator, the memory comes flooding back to me like a hurricane. All I see are the dark waves of the abyss coming toward me, and the uncomfortable feeling that it will swallow me up soon. This would be the one moment when I turned my back on the waves. The problem was, I didn't even know I was at the beach.

When my mom died, it seemed so odd that the sun rose every morning and went down every night. I hadn't been sure it would if my mother was not there. She was the sick one, yet the strong one. And she was taken away from me. "Don't bite the hand that feeds you," she would say. *Well, Mom, what happens when that nurturing hand disappears altogether?* My problems were bigger than my shoe size, which was gearing up to be a 9.

I was sitting in my room that day, writing in my diary—the diary that my mom had purchased for me so I could express my feelings. I oftentimes picture her browsing our local Crown Books, combing through the diaries with pickable locks, hoping her young daughter would write about the difficulties of being seven or eight years old, but knowing better. Knowing that her diary would be wrapped up in woes that would never be solved —and that in fact were bound to get worse. And she would be right. I never had the luxury of writing entries about meeting a boy, or going to Disneyland, or that I was so in love with Jonathan Taylor Thomas. I penned entries that ached with heartbreak and longed for change. I just didn't know what that change was, and I was too young to have expected what would come next.

My dad was cold to me in the days after. He was his regular sentimental self when we sat shivah, but there was something else brewing inside him. We had no way of anticipating how he would react to my mom's death. I only wish we had. My parents' wedding album mysteriously disappeared the follow-ing year, the year my sister got engaged. My mom's other belongings—the contents of the walk-in closet—simply van-ished into thin air. No one has ever taken responsibility for these items' whereabouts.

That last afternoon before we sat shivah, he bellowed to me from his room down the hall, no more than twenty feet away from mine. My mom had been dead for only six days at that point. I reluctantly walked across the beige carpet, hoping he was in a better mood than I thought. I felt the floorboards creak below me, and for a moment I secretly regretted I was on top of them. If we had a basement, I could have hidden there.

As I entered my parents' room, I looked down at the floor. My heart stopped. Pain surged up into my throat—the kind of pain that causes you to choke up and makes your eyes water with tears that hit your sinuses like a shot of saline; sadly, a familiar feeling to me. All of my mom's clothes were strewn on the floor. The place was a mess, resembling a crowded outlet store. But this was no outlet store, and these clothes objectified all I had left of my mother's physical possessions.

"Daddy, what are you doing?" I would ask that question repeatedly for a few more weeks and months. "I'm not ready to get rid of her stuff." Throughout my life, I used to play in her walk-in closet, going through her pumps, her jewelry, and her memories. I wasn't ready to put all of that in white trash bags and haul them over to the women's shelter. This wasn't spring cleaning—she was my mom. As a twelve-year-old who had just lost the only constant love she knew, I knew all I had of her were these items inside her closet. And now my father was throwing them on the floor.

"Dad, stop! Please!" I was sobbing but also in panic mode, jumping on the floor, trying to salvage whatever I could. But I didn't know where anything was that I might have wanted to save. He had rifled through her daily order of getting ready, something she cherished so much.

Far back in a very dark corner of my mind, I remember my dad telling me at this moment, that my mom had cheated on him with a man named Frank Parker before I was born. Why he deemed it appropriate to tell me this is beyond me, but as a human being, I remember feeling sorry for him, and I wanted to listen. I wanted to be supportive.

I can still hear the sound of plastic hangers hitting one another onto the bedroom floor. Even today, every time I enter a dry cleaner, I can't bear to hear the hangers clattering together. The sound pulls me right back to this moment.

I expect no one knew, but when my mother was still alive, every time the cleaning lady was done with the bathroom my parent's shared, I sometimes sneaked into her walk-in closet and inhaled her perfume, touched her clothes, and looked at her hats. Why she had hats was beyond me. They were on the top shelf, and she never wore them. Since she'd died, they were also that certain something that made me remember that my mother, whom I had just lost, had been human. Just a week earlier, she had been living. She had been a person who bought hats and never wore them. She had been a person who wore Rive Gauche perfume by Yves Saint Laurent. She had been a person who was madly in love with someone she had not married. She was flawed yet perfect. She was troubled, at times, but real. She did not always know what the right thing to do was, so she sometimes bought hats she never wore.

"No, Dad, don't throw all of it away, she would have wanted it donated," I said.

But I recall him saying he did not care what she wanted. My dad quickly became someone I did not recognize following the days after my mom's death. It seemed as though he wanted all of her possessions to disappear—as if he hadn't just lost a wife, but instead been stood up on Prom night.

I grabbed a T-shirt that had some French writing on it that my mom used to tuck into jeans, pulling a skinny, white leather strap around her waist. I think she wore it to Disneyland once. I took the T-shirt and ran. To this day, it's the only article of clothing I have of hers. And I can still hear the hangers clattering.

J'm wide-awake in a strange room that is tattered with white and beige paint streaks. Faux painting, my mom would have corrected me. I know somewhere nearby, there are hangers. There is nothing in the room except a bed, the large, gold-infused mirror I oftentimes use as a vanity, and white sheets streaming across the hardwood floor. I'm waiting for someone, but I don't know for whom. I'm lying in a bed that is decorated with my sister's bedding: tan and white sheets coursing like ribbons over my body. I'm looking at old photo albums, and suddenly I see pictures of my parents' wedding, but not their wedding that took place in the 1970s, overlooking the ocean on a lush, green bluff. It was a wedding that took place more recently—in 2001. My mother was wearing a deep-purple gown that electrified her bright green eyes, and my father was wearing a snazzy blue suit. As I turn the pages of the photo album, I suddenly feel that I'm not alone. She's next to me. She's looking over my shoulder.

"Mom? What are you doing here?" I ask, truly puzzled. She

just smiles; she won't say anything to me. And then it happens —I am submerged in the photo album; I am thrust into the memory. I'm suddenly at my parents' second wedding. They are holding each other cheek to cheek in the middle of a banquet room on a cruise ship comparable in looks and build to the *Queen Mary*. Are we docked? I don't think so. I am wearing lavender to complement my mother's purple gown and seeing a bunch of people who are no longer alive.

"Robin? Is that you?" Robin has been dead for five years. He had been one of my parents' best friends. He just smiles at me as he weaves through the crowd of guests in fancy clothes, not saying a word. I look at my parents—they seem so happy. They're about to take their vows. They want privacy, so I begin to usher the guests up a grand staircase to the rooftop of the vessel, where the party will take place. The stairs are extremely steep, and the boat is constantly rocking. I grip the ivory rails with white knuckles. The ocean is beyond my control at this point—after all, I am on it, not in it.

Robin opens the door to the roof, and I see below us throttling waves that look like they might take this gigantic vessel out. "Wait, Robin," I say. He doesn't hear me. *No one seems to hear me. Am I the dead one instead?* And then I look down at my parents and time has stopped. They are frozen—glitter looks almost to be encapsulating them, like in a Disney film. Drama fills the room, like when the last rose petal falls in *Beauty and the Beast. Will the Beast survive? Where is Belle to break the spell?*

"What is happening?" I say out loud, as I rush past the guests to get to my parents. Why are they frozen? I can't reach them. A force field is blocking me. I put my hand out and hit an invisible wall, and then it's all understood: My mother is sick again. The wedding cannot go on.

I AM BACK IN THE STRANDED ROOM, lying next to my mother in bed, with the photo album in my hands. Tears form in my eyes, and I look at her. Her once perfectly red nails are stricken with fungus. "You have to find a way to make our vows real, Jessica," she says to me.

"Mom, how can I do that? You're sick. Your vows stopped." This was some unspoken understanding that makes sense only in the deepest of dreams: If you're sick, your vows don't go through. If you're sick, you die too soon.

"You have to make them go through this time."

"Mom," I say, stroking her blond hair, "you're already married to Dad—this was just a second time around. So, see, it really doesn't matter that time froze. You are married to Dad."

"No, I'm not. It ends in death. Till death do us part."

"Yes, you are." We are mother and daughter bickering in a random bed, the sheets now covering both of us. Are we dead or alive? My mom smells like Caress Body Wash, like she has just taken a long bath and used her favorite bright orange loofah. She starts crying.

"Jessica, please help me."

"Mom, I can't make you better. I never could."

"You can do this for me—I know you can."

"Do what?"

"Make the vows real, or else you can never get married. You can't get married until I'm married."

My heart sinks. I thought they were married. Aren't they? I want to be married. How do I do the impossible so I can finally save my mother, and myself?

***

I CANCEL AN APPOINTMENT that I never ordinarily would to be with my mom, because I know she would be dead when I came back. We finally get to speak to each other as two women —not as a little girl and a scared young mother. We are equals, and I still can't save her. She continues to cry, telling me, "You think I'm unhappy because I'm sick and that I have no reason to live, but I do. I'm happy. I'm happy with your father."

I shake my head as if I agree with her, but I truly don't. I truly cannot understand her right now.

"Don't pity me, Jessica." I stare into her deep-green eyes for a long time, and then, in the blink of an eye, she's gone. She left me again. Scared and sad, I go downstairs and see my grandmother in a hospital bed, hoping that I can save her, even though she's much older than my mom.

And then I hear a noise: the loud screech of a garbage truck and the soft hum of a vacuum in the apartment upstairs. I wake up and recognize my large mirror, which had journeyed into the dream with me. I am no longer in this barren room with my mother; I am completely alone, and I still didn't save her. "Mom?" I look around the room and get my diary out. "I better write this one down," I mutter to myself.

And so day number 210 of my investigation begins. I get out of bed alone, I brush my teeth alone, and I go to make sense of my mother's long-lost life without her. I look into the gold mirror, agonizing over every pore. I always think of my mom when I look at my pores and notice fine lines around my mouth, because these are both genetic. It's all I have to hold on to. I took a five-question quiz in *Cosmopolitan* once that said I have medium-size pores and the potential to have the same-size laugh lines, like she did. And so goes another day in my life: still motherless and always will be, no matter how much research I do.

Eleven years have passed, and it is not easy to do what I have chosen. Most people would assume that when a great maternal figure dies, the whole family comes together and honors her with their closeness. That is not so much my reality. For all emotional intents and purposes, my family scattered into the forest. We all have mourned and missed my mom on our own, all alone. And I am past that point. My mom's death is the one thing that I've been able to be strong about and move on from. And I have trusted the future with her. I have trusted that our relationship would find a way to grow from beyond the grave. I always trusted that she was around me, teaching me through other people, showing me the way. She would have been an outstanding, living mother to me because she was similar to me. She was a free spirit, too. I will know how to raise one of us. After all, she still is a free spirit—a beautiful butterfly, frolicking from one petal groove to another.

This investigation is my love letter to her life and our relationship, which never quite bloomed. I can remember feeling ugly and gawky when I was young, and when my mother looked at me, I felt beautiful all of a sudden. She could put the entire world right side up for me. Her sickness made me question God, question a higher power, and feel as if the walls were closing in on me. I had no choice but to forfeit my relationship with my mother. A good friend in college told me, "God took away someone so close to you at such a tender age. He will surely give it back to you in many ways." I like to believe that when I am sad. But I mostly believe that my mom is here with me, always. She will give it back to me somehow. As I have learned time and again on this journey, Dianne always pulls through.

*I*n the car, my mom sang along with "Twist and Shout," The Beatles version, and I replied with weak backup vocals, too shy to sing the whole chorus myself. My mom continued, letting the silver Volvo station wagon dance by pumping the brakes to the beat as we waited for the light to turn green. I was late for dance class. It was my first time trying lyrical, and I was really nervous.

"Loosen up, Jess—here's your part," my mom talked-sang, holding up a fake microphone to my lips. She started, moving it back toward her.

"Ahhhh," I blushed and sang. "Ahhhhh, ahhhhh, owwww!"

"You did it!" she shouted, laughing, her green eyes sparkling in the sun. I always thought my mom didn't wear sunglasses so all the world could see her striking eyes, but it turned out today she had just forgotten them.

Turning onto Jeffrey Street, my mom pointed to the orange groves to my right. "We really need to go pick some oranges before they cut them down," she said. "Orange County is really expanding into something else." I looked around, seeing a few people collecting bags of oranges. We never went and picked oranges.

Oh no, I thought. We were almost at dance class. I started to bite my nails, a bad habit that to this day I can't seem to quit. "Stop biting, Jess," my mom ordered. "I'm going to get that gross-tasting polish so that every time you go to bite, you'll be disgusted."

"Yum," I responded sarcastically. My mom squealed a little and turned up the radio. "Yes! It must be Beatles hour or something. I love this song!" She sang happily, periodically doing the four-clap when we hit a red light.

She pointed out that she and her friends used to do two claps up and then two claps down. It was four-clap protocol, clearly. I happily sang along. I really liked this song, for some reason. Not as much as 98 Degrees or NSYNC, however.

My new dance teacher, Sarah, was in the window, demonstrating pliés, as we turned into the shopping center where the Dance Academy was. Having been a tapper since the age of three, I was nervous to try lyrical, since it was more modern and demanded more flexibility, strength, and classical technique. My foundation was weak. "You'll do fine, Jess," my mom reassured me. "You were born to dance."

"Bye, Mommy. See you in an hour," I said, rushing out of the car in my purple leotard. Did people wear leotards to lyrical? I wasn't sure.

"I'm going over to Scott's to see if he can't do something about my terrible roots, but I'll be back to get you! Kisses," she said.

I closed the door and ran into class. Everyone stared at me in my purple leotard. I have to say, I always loved dance but despised the girls I danced with. My teacher, Sarah, however, was perfect by my standards. Tall and lean, with long blond hair, she wore the totally best dance pants ever; I envied her. *She must have the perfect life*, my eight-year-old mind thought. Of course, my idea of a perfect life included anyone who did not have a dying mother in her forties who had enough life in her soul to start a Beatles concert in the car.

I WAS IN FOURTH GRADE that year, in an advanced class for smart kids. Constantly changing schools was my MO, beginning at age seven. I think my mother wanted my life to be perfect; and the second something went wrong (things inevitably go wrong in elementary school), she would make me switch schools. People thought I moved houses a lot, but my dad still lives in the house I grew up in. We never moved.

This particular time, my mom thought it would be best for me to take this opportunity and enroll in the APPAS program at Eastshore Elementary. There, we learned more advanced and worldly things than regular fourth graders did. By the middle of the year, I had learned the skill of mnemonic memory devices and had memorized all of the U.S. presidents in order of their terms and could recite all fifty states in alphabetical order to a rather catchy tune. I also learned sign language, had to participate in the science fair (even though at other schools it started in fifth grade), and was the witch in the school play of *Hansel and Gretel*.

The most memorable moment about fourth grade, however,

was the poetry contest around Mother's Day, put on by a local jewelry store, Gallery of Diamonds. The student who wrote the most outstanding poem won a diamond for his or her mother. The year before, at my regular school, I had won my mom an African garnet, which she had made into a necklace for me, but this year I was determined to put up a better fight. I would come out guns a-blazing. Poetry was always a strong suit of mine and a stronger suit of my mother's. To my mom, I was bursting with creativity.

My mother was terminally ill with countless autoimmune diseases derived from her weakened immune system from all the cancer treatments over the years. Some weeks and months were better than others. Her health could change daily, and it distracted me from my schoolwork. For my sister, homework was grounding. For me, I had come to experience worrying about my mom as an acquired comfort. I was so accustomed to my life being an emotional merry-go-round that when my parents went out to dinner, I worried they would never come back. If I could not reach them on their beeper, I cried to my Italian grandmother, Ann.

My grandmother would pray to some saint that my parents were safe. Saint Anthony. "Please, Saint Anthony, bring them back safely," she would say, looking up to the sky—or, rather, to this Anthony person. We did not have saints in Judaism, so I was very confused about this topic. I thought Jesus was the only one they cared about. *Oh well*, I thought. My rabbi would be disappointed to know that this tactic worked like a charm. The phone would ring shortly after the prayer to St. Anthony, and it would be my mom answering my page: "Your father didn't hear it again. Sorry, Jess," she would say. Or my parents would come in the door, looking very excited to see me. I can still remember the way my mother's big winter coat smelled, mixing with the scents of the restaurant they had gone to that night and her perfume.

Since my mom's health was always up in the air, I had to be truly thankful for the days she could get up and go out to dinner and then come home and watch *Saturday Night Live* with me. My mom could empathize with my fear of her not returning or not being all right. I later learned that she suffered through those same feelings, without any real cause, with her own mother. I like to think, although she might have found it annoying at times, that this trait of worrying about our parents' mortality distinguished me as similar to her and therefore made her happy. I was incredibly aware of my surroundings and the inherent consequences of life.

On this particular night, though, I had to finish my poem for the contest; submissions were due the next day. My sister had just begun college, so she was out of the house, and my father was asleep. It was just my mom and myself, downstairs in our pajamas, trying to brainstorm and finish this poem. She was writing random words and quotes and images on a large yellow legal pad. I stared at her, in total and complete writer's block. "I don't know what to write, Mom." I furrowed my brows.

"Stop doing that—you'll get wrinkles," she warned me. "This is supposed to be fun, Jess! Come on, now."

"Okay, fine. My mom is a cozy place. That's all I have," I said. Because my mother had a newfound love of similes, she responded, "Like a warm cup of cocoa . . . and what rhymes with 'place'?"

"'Lace,'" I exclaimed.

"That's a pretty word, Jess. Do you want some cocoa?" she asked, getting up to make some. She loved snacks late at night but would never admit it if you asked her. "No, thanks. You never buy the kind with the marshmallows anymore," I responded.

"Like a warm cup of cocoa or a pillow trimmed with lace," my mom recited. Then she excused herself to go the bathroom. I got up and talked to her through the cracks in the bathroom door.

"Enough with the metaphors," I said, thinking that I was not Shakespeare. "My mom's love is all mine, I can always depend," I said. "You're more than just my mom." She came out of the bathroom.

"She's my best friend," she said warmly, with a smile, drying her hands on a peach hand towel. In one half-hour session, my mother and I had come up with a simple yet sweet and true poem. She probably was not supposed to help me, but I thought of her as more of a collaborator than a cowriter. As it goes, here was the poem—no edits and no frills:

> My mom is a cozy place
> Like a warm cup of cocoa
> Or a pillow trimmed with lace
> My mom's love is all mine
> I can always depend
> She's more than a mom, she's my best friend.

The next day at school, I submitted my handwritten—in cursive, of course—Mother's Day poem. It was ready to go in a large manila envelope that was to be mailed to the Gallery of Diamonds that afternoon. I looked around the room, wondering what the other kids had come up with. My poem seemed to be the shortest, but it surely was not a haiku or something.

To my left, I saw an Asian kid whom I had known since I was three. His mom was in the room, collecting the poems, and seemed surprised at how short my entry looked. I tried to ignore her gaze, and also tried to ignore the constant gazes of the kids who had known me most of my life and knew that sometimes my mom picked me up from school with oxygen tubes in her nose, stemming from a large green tank in the backseat. "Is that your grandma?" a moronic boy named Ryan once asked me. I ran to the back of the playground and burst into tears before I got into the car. No, that was not my grandma.

Why couldn't I have a regular mom? Why did she have to be so sick? Half the time I really didn't know what was wrong with her. Most people who know sick people can say "breast cancer" with a frown, or "leukemia" with large, sad eyes and a shrug. I could not do that. My mom had already survived non-Hodgkin's lymphoma and a stubborn thymoma by the time I was eight years old. In fact, she had survived the lymphoma five years before I was even conceived. I could not comprehend how someone could survive cancer twice, be on so many rounds of chemotherapy, take so many pills per day, and still be so very sick.

I learned the word "terminal" at quite a young age. Walking down the green, grassy hill toward my mom's station wagon, seeing the oxygen tubes in her nose and knowing it must be a bad day for her made me realize something that I would struggle with my whole life. Nothing is forever. Nothing is guaranteed. Not your health. Not your happiness. And definitely not your mom.

"Is it all right for you to be driving like that?" I asked her.

"Of course, Jess. How was school?" The interesting thing about people being sick in society is that they carry a certain calling card with them. It's not like a policeman could have ticketed her for driving under the influence. In my mom's condition, it was more like driving under normal influence, and once the cop saw her young daughter in the car, he wouldn't care. He would simply nod, call home just to say hi, and thank the Lord his fortysomething wife was not sick and driving her child around with a pet oxygen tank in the backseat.

My fourth grade teacher knew that my mom was ill, although my mom hid it as much as she possibly could. There was a reality of my going to school, and missing school, for that matter. The days my mom was too sick, I just wanted to stay at home with her, or, if she was in the hospital, to stay with my grandmother and cry on her lap. I didn't know when things would get better. I never did.

One day we could be joking around, drinking hot cocoa in the kitchen, writing a poem, and the next she could be unable to breathe on her own and have to be put on life support. An ambulance would come take my mother away. I didn't know if I would ever see her again. The worst part about her being on life support—by that, I mean having a tube down her throat and letting a machine breathe for her—was that I could not go and see her. At least when she was in a regular room, we could all have dinner together or I could bring her a card or flowers. But when she was on life support, I wouldn't see her for weeks at a time. I was too young to go into the intensive care unit. She would write me notes. Oftentimes she would be up in Los Angeles, because that was where her oncologists were, and my sister, who was attending UCLA at the time, would dutifully go and do her homework while sitting next to my mom on the breathing machine. They would pass notes to each other and share smiles and muted laughter. I remember being jealous that my sister got to be with her and I didn't.

Can you imagine? At eight or nine, I wished only that I could be in the intensive care unit of Cedars-Sinai hospital, spending time with my terminally ill mother. I did not want to go to Disneyland or play miniature golf like the other kids. I wanted to be with my mother. She was my prize, my token for getting a good grade on a history test, my diamond in the rough.

My mom had been doing well for the few weeks following the poem. We were in the process of redecorating our very 1980s-style home decor, and actually lived in the local Marriott for a period of time because the whole house was being gutted. This was the time before CD players were in cars, and one of the times we were going back to the Marriott from school, my mom told me she had a new song for me to hear that I would love. It was from the man who sang "Jack & Diane."

"John Mellencamp?" I questioned, always knowing what my mom's favorite music was at any given point. "You got it, honey bunny. Take a listen," she said with a wink. I tried to listen to the lyrics and judge the music, like she taught me to.

My mom was quite the music enthusiast. She claimed to have been at various Beatles and Elvis concerts when she was young. Once, when my sister was making a video about 1968 for her high school history class, we could have sworn we saw my mom and her best friend, Donna, on some footage from a Beatles show in Los Angeles. "Did you go to Woodstock?" I asked, not quite understanding that Woodstock was in upstate New York and not as accessible as it is now. As I listened to "Cherry Bomb," I quickly understood why my mom was so fond of the song. The lyrics spoke of being a young girl, falling in love, and living for herself. And dancing. Something she did not get to do anymore—*or did she ever?* I wondered.

My mom was a gourmet cook when she wasn't focusing all her attention on surviving the day. At the time, she was perfecting her stuffed-bell-pepper dish of the month. I remember coming home from school one day during the week of Halloween and smelling baked apples outside the front door. I walked in, wearing my Puffy Paint-decorated Halloween shirt with a big jack-o'-lantern on the front, and was greeted with baked stuffed apples, a treat that Ethel, my mom's mom, often made for her as a little girl.

"Want to pour the cinnamon on top?" my mom asked, her bright green eyes beaming. "Sure," I exclaimed, my hands sweaty and dirty from school, with that feeling that only playing on monkey bars at a playground could leave you with. "Wash your hands, please," she said, pointing to the kitchen sink. My eyes then fixated on the thirteen-by-nine Pyrex pan that encased six enlarged Roma apples stuffed with caramel and breadcrumbs.

As my mom helped me pour the cinnamon on top with the sifter, I felt lucky for the first time in a long time. My life seemed quite normal at that point, but it would be only a week later when my friend's mother had to take me to the dentist because my mom was in the hospital in Los Angeles. I got to join the

No-Cavity Club for the first time that visit, without a parent present. I was so excited—excited but lonely, too, for I had no one to share the moment with. So much of the time other people were raising me, and while I knew that wasn't in my mother's control, I could not help but feel robbed of a real childhood. I felt a constant longing. Much of the time that she was alive I missed her as if she were already gone.

During the last month of fourth grade, we were supposed to find out whether we had placed in the poetry contest. We did not find out in school who had won; rather, you received a letter or a phone call directly from the jewelry store if you placed high enough. I came home from school one day to my mom hanging up the phone with a huge smile on her face.

"Jess, guess what?"

I shook my head, as to say, *I don't know what; tell me.* Nothing too exciting ever happened to a fourth grader, so I assumed it was something like I didn't have Sunday school that weekend (I hated getting up early, even though I did get to eat donuts beforehand). I looked up at my mom and said, "What is it?"

"You won! Your poem got first place. You won me a diamond."

A real, tingling shock coursed through my body for the first time. Maybe I *could* be a writer one day if I really wanted to be. I looked down at my matching purple-and-pink outfit from the kids' department and wondered if one day I would be wearing Versace while writing for *Cosmopolitan*. But for now, I was Orange County's contest-winning poet who had just won a diamond for her mom on Mother's Day.

"Wow!" I exclaimed. Tearing up while running to my mom

and holding her tightly yet gently, I felt time stop. She had an artificial trachea at that point, and I did not want to knock the stopper out of the silver hole, because that would have temporarily left her unable to breathe and speak. "Better safe than sorry" was always my childhood motto.

A few weeks later, my mom was well enough to attend the ceremony at which I received the diamond for her. Much to my surprise, the jeweler handed me a royal-blue velvet box. I thought it was going to be a single, perfect diamond for my mother—after all, it was her birthstone—but it wasn't. Inside the delicate box were two diamond studs. Perfect for my eight-year-old ears. My eyes widened.

Unfortunately, money was often tight during this time, as the medical insurance coverage toward the end of my mother's life was not reliable. "Do you like them, Jess?" I nodded fervently. "We had them split the diamond in two. I have enough diamonds your father has given me, and you earned this."

"Mommy, thank you so much!"

"You deserve it, Sheynah Meydeleh. You deserve it all." The afternoon flew by, as we were interviewed by the *Orange Country Register* and photographed at a few different angles. My mom wore a green scarf to cover up her trachea, and I felt so proud. Not once did my mom mention that we had collaborated on this poem; she bragged to her friends on the phone about me and insisted that I had done all the work. Only in my heart did I ever share the joy and credit with her. In my eyes, she saw the successful writer I might become, and in my eyes, all I saw was a beautiful diamond in the rough.

JESSICA

Fall 2011

ear Diary,

I've never had such a hard September. Tonight I remember my mom. I remember her always. And while I'm so grateful for all that she gave me, I wish she were here so badly it kills me. I want her to meet my husband. I want her to hold my child. I want her to hold me. I don't want to sell a book because I lost her. I wish I just had her. Sometimes I don't want my story—I just want my mom. But my story is all I have.

I just want my mom. I want her to know me. I want to sing the Beatles in the car with her. I want to watch a movie with her. I want her to stroll through the park with me. I want her to look at me. I miss her so much it hurts. I miss what I knew and what I never will know. I miss seeing a future with my mother. I hope, I pray, that I can build a family she would be proud of and fit into. I don't want to raise my family in a home that's unrecognizable to her. I know she's with me, but she can't talk to me.

I want her to tell me what's right from wrong. I want her to squeeze my hand and tuck me in. I want to show all the love I don't get to show her anymore. I want to show it to someone special. I don't want to be alone anymore. I want to love despite her, through her, because of her. Twelve years. I never thought this day would come. I have now spent more of my life without her than with her. I feel her essence in every single thing I do. I see her sly grin in my big smile. I see her flirtatious expression in my wink. Just keep believing, Mom, keep being here with me. I need you. I don't want to be toyed with, I want to be loved. I'm ready.

I wish I had one day with you. One hour. One minute. One pearl of wisdom. I wish you could lock eyes with me and notice the woman I've become. Don't leave me. Not again.

Jessica

I LEARNED AT A YOUNG AGE—and not just from Nancy Drew books—that secrets are everywhere. I think of the day I realized Carolyn Keene was a pseudonym: the name was actually just a pen name that several authors used to write countless mysteries with the same characters. My mother and I used to take trips to the local Barnes & Noble to browse the young-adult section and buy the latest Nancy Drew mystery book, which is an anomaly, as there were not any "new" Nancy Drew books, because they all had been written decades before. Each book just seemed new to me.

I found out about Carolyn Keene's pseudonym when I was in the middle of writing fan mail to her. My mom kindly told me she could not be contacted. I immediately closed the Micro-soft Word document and shed a tear for Miss Keene. All these

Miss Keenes would never know that they had inspired me to be an investigative journalist. The collaborative part of it inspires me still, however. They must at least have had the same editor.

Speaking of secrets, my mother's entire past was a secret to me. Who was she thinking of all those lonely nights in the hospital when death was looming and it was past my bedtime? I knew almost nothing of her past, only secrets she whispered or stories she began and could not finish. Letters from her estranged best friend she read in private. Old pictures she blushed while looking at and then quickly tucked away, like a scared mouse scurrying back into its hiding place. The only pieces of information I knew came from her telling me: she grew up in Westchester, California; lived there for a period of time; fell in love on the beach once with a boy who later died in Vietnam; worked at Lawry's Prime Rib in West Hollywood in the '70s and early '80s; and had as her ballroom dance partner Frank Parker, whom she apparently loved well past the dancing years.

Questions about who she was haunted me throughout my adolescence and followed me to college, where one of my journalism professors, who is a Pulitzer Prize winner and well known for his career in writing compelling obituaries, taught me that you *can* tell someone else's story after they're gone— but only if people are willing to talk. Suddenly, I was inspired to journey through my mom's past via the people who knew her during each phase of her life: her teenage years, her young adulthood, and her romantic relationships.

I TAKE A LONG BREATH and blow hair up through my side bangs. *When is class out?* I am in the middle of a media theory class, and my mind is elsewhere. It's the fourteenth of September, I realize, and my heart sinks. I drum my fingernails on the table in front of me and look out the window of journalism class. I stare at the clock's display, 2:42 p.m., willing it to change. I have to get out of here. Suddenly, a memory comes flooding back. I am in Lakeside Middle School, and it's 1999. I am in my seventh-grade algebra class.

In 1999, my home life was not typical, to say the least. I had just started menstruating for the first time. My uncle Harvey happened to be with me. Unfortunately there were no women present, so I had to go the pharmacy with him and buy Kotex pads, and as I was wandering through the aisles, I knew how much easier it would have been to be there with my mom. Harvey bought me not one but two different kinds of nail polish out of sheer sadness, I think. My mom was not dead— she was incapacitated in a nursing home, her brain not functioning properly because of the spinal fluid that had traveled there from her meningitis. To stay afloat, I had just spent half of sixth grade living with a former teacher of mine, because my mother was ill at home. Physically removing myself from the situation was the easiest thing I ever did; knowing when it would end was the hardest part.

One night, I was about to be picked up to go to a movie, and the phone rang. My grandma Ann answered it. My heart sank—I knew who it was. "It's your mother, Jess. Come talk to her." Talking to my mom was horrifically sad for me. She did not know who she was most of the time, during the last six months of her life.

"Hello," I said timidly.

"It rained last night. Did you hear it? I thought of you." My heart broke into a million pieces. Of course I had thought of her, too. Rain was our thing. I choked up. "Jess? Did you think of me?"

I nodded first, and my grandma saw me starting to cry, so she rubbed my arm and said, "Tell her, honey," in her calming New York accent.

"Yeah, of course, Mommy."

"I hope to see you soon," she said. Visiting her was hard—my forty-nine-year-old mother was in a nursing home, talking to the pet birds and not knowing who she was 90 percent of the time. This moment would be the only time in the last year of her life when she remembered who she was and that she was my mom.

Back to seventh grade—Algebra was almost over. I felt extreme relief, and then a shock rushed over me as I thought of my mom, lying alone in the hospital bed, not knowing where she was or who she was. I closed my eyes for a moment and felt a hand over my heart and a rush of tears to my eyeballs. For a minute there, time stopped. I didn't know what had just happened, but school was to get out in three minutes. I was worried. I knew something was wrong, but I had lived twelve years, long enough, with a sick mother, and so I knew that panic does nothing. I walked calmly to my locker and got my things. As I waited for my friend's mother to pick me up, I climbed a large, grassy hill to watch for her arrival.

After I got into my friend's car, I had a silent ride home. I just wanted to get home. I knew my sister or my father would be home, even though it was a school and work day. "Thanks for the ride," I yelled back at my friend's mother as I put on my pink JanSport backpack and then rang the doorbell, as I often did when I was scrambling to find the house key. My mother taught me always to be polite, even when you don't really like people.

My sister opened the door with the phone in her hand. Tears were streaming down her face. When my sister cries, I cry; it's like a reflex when the pediatrician taps your knee and your calf goes flying upward beyond your control. I began to tear up as her nearly never unsteady arm wavered. She dropped the portable phone on the ground, and time seemed to slow down. My eyes followed it midair and watched it crash and break. The tiny white buttons separated from their respective covers. A flat dial tone filled the air. I didn't try to put the pieces back together.

"What now?" I asked. I thought I was unfazed by hysterics and all the drama that constantly filled my life. One minute, my mom was fine and making Bisquick pancakes; the next, she was on a ventilator in the intensive care unit.

"She's gone." My mother was dead.

The days following and the funeral were a blur. To this day, I can't remember who belonged to the crying faces of the people who gave me condolence hugs, or the eyes full of sympathy for my family and me. All I remember is that I wore the Mary Janes I had purchased with my mother, and, after getting cemetery dirt on their soles, never wore them again. My sister spoke, my two uncles spoke, and my rabbi gave a eulogy, too. I don't remember what anyone said—I just felt numb. To be honest, I think I cried harder at my sister's wedding.

I don't know if it was shock, or the fact that the nightmare was finally over, or a combination of the two, but we were all relieved. We were mad at ourselves for being relieved. We were embarrassed to be in this situation and unsure of how to live without the comfortable burden we had grown so accustomed to. We were sad with her, and sad without her. Having never had a normal upbringing, I looked at my mother's coffin and realized something: I was alone, and I would now always be motherless. I could not focus on the sadness. I was concerned about high school and boyfriends and all the rest of the world that was left up to me to figure out. How would I manage? Would I succeed? Would I thrive? Would I be alone? Would I be okay? How could she leave me? How had this happened? I thought if I anticipated the waves and never let problems sneak up on me, everything would be okay. I guess the ocean rules don't always apply to life—or maybe they just don't apply to death.

I deduced that I was numb at my mother's funeral mostly because I was worried about myself. It took me over twenty years to realize that I was not totally alone, that I created the blessings I have, but some days it is still hard for me to accept. It is hard for me to justify, and hard for me to stomach. I was always dreaming of someone swooping down from the sky and taking my pain away. The old soul in me wondered: Would I put that pressure on a man? Did she put that pressure on a man? Was she happy with her life? How could she have been? It ended too soon. I had a brief idea of how she grew up but did not know specifics. Was there something I'd missed?

*W*hen I finally set out on my quest to uncover my mother's past, my first witness was her lifelong confidant, Audrey Neller. I had known Audrey as an elderly woman, but before this she had been a schoolteacher in Westchester, my mom's hometown.

"Whatever happened to Audrey?" I asked my grandma. She and Audrey had both lived in the retirement community, Leisure World, until recently when my grandma had moved in with us.

Leisure World was the retirement community that my grandmother had lived in for twenty years. I use the term "retirement" loosely, as those old people did everything but retire. There were two thousand different clubs they could join, various sports contests and entertainment shows and "dinner dances," as my grandma called them, to attend, and a mall close by where they could shop. There were buses that drove approximately three miles per hour and went all around the different "gates" that spanned the community. It was always a joke that if your name was not listed at the "gate" then the elderly gatekeeper would call the office, and then the police, on you. One time they did that to my mom because she didn't have her pass out, and she had to pull around and wait forty-five minutes for one of us to come prove her identity. Jason Bourne would have had trouble getting into Leisure World if the right eighty-year-old guard had been on duty that day. Nevertheless, my grandma loved her life there and, most of all, her friends. Audrey was one of them.

Audrey Neller was a New York City transplant who lived three houses down from my mother in Westchester, on Anise Avenue. She had one daughter and suffered from polio for several years of her life. Audrey was very close to Ethel, my grandmother, back in the 1950s, and as my mother grew into an adult, Audrey grew close to her, too. When my family moved to Orange County from Los Angeles, and Audrey moved from Westchester to Leisure World, we joined the same temple, Temple Bat Yahm. I am not sure how my mother and Audrey became so close. Perhaps it was because Ethel passed away when my mom was just thirty-nine years old, or that my mother was so sick and Audrey was familiar with suffering at a young age. Or maybe it was because they shared a love of fashion, style, charm, and a great laugh that they were automatically drawn together. From the time I was a little girl, I always thought of Audrey as a surrogate grandmother to me.

I actually thought I had four grandmothers because my mom was fond of so many elderly ladies. I had Grandma Ann, my real, Italian grandma; Grandma Evelyn, my mom's childhood live-in maid who used to knit me colorful blankets every holiday season; Grandma Ethel, who passed away before I could get to know her; and Grandma Audrey, who just seemed to fit our family the best. I can see Audrey right now, walking into Rosh Hashanah services, wearing a large yellow hat and matching yellow suit. She would carry a beige bag and have nude-looking shoes to match, as a city girl's bag must always match her shoes. That is how you pull the look together. "Hi, darling," Audrey would say in a raspy, heavy New York accent. "You look fabulous, Di!" She called my mom Di because my mother really resembled Princess Di. She would kiss my mom's cheek and then slip me a hard candy just in case I got bored during the rabbi's sermon.

I could always spot Audrey, with her platinum-blond hair and colorful, encrusted broaches that I secretly yearned for. They had emeralds, rubies, pearls, and diamonds on them. I used to try to touch them. The things four-year-old little girls can get away with. "My darling Jessica," Audrey would say. "Look at that puttum face!" Audrey always smelled like Chanel No. 5 and baby powder. When she took her hat off, her hair would be pulled up into a high French twist. Everything about her was very Manhattan. She had grown up in the city and lived there until she met her husband at graduate school in Chicago. I never knew her husband, Norm, too well. Their answering machine greeting was, "You've reached the Nellers. Lucky you! Leave us a message." Sometimes Audrey wore a neck brace, as her polio still debilitated her joints at random.

When I thought of Audrey or spent time with her, I always considered her independence and ability to make everyone around her love her, and laugh while doing so. Her charm was unlike anyone else's. She would go visit my mother in the hospital, taking her flowers, and would send her gifts when she was recuperating at home. In 2010, I found a present Audrey sent my mom. It was a "bosom pouch," and attached was a sweet note that read: "Hi Di, use this to keep your boobs cozy." My mother and Audrey shared a trait that not many have: they both exuded confidence and beauty that were regal and commanding. I always thought that my mom wanted to look and act like Audrey when she aged, but she never got the chance to.

Once I really committed to doing research, I dedicated my time to finding Audrey once and for all. I received her daughter's number through a close family friend and, one day in June, decided to call her up. Her daughter's name was Lesley, and she went to Westchester High School with my mother. Lesley ended up being much more of an important contact than I had ever thought I could possibly find. My first question was obvious: "What happened to your mom? Is she still alive?" I felt so embarrassed asking that. I was twisting my green pillowcase around my fingers out of nervousness, and I could feel my cheeks flush, regretting in one instant all the years that had slipped between now and the last time I had seen Audrey. *My mom must be so disappointed*, I thought.

"She's still alive," Lesley answered. "But she's not the Audrey you remember. She's on hospice and living in a board-and-care home."

"I want to see her," I stated.

"I don't know if you want to do that—"

"I do," I interrupted her. All of a sudden, I felt a surge of energy to do whatever possible to see Audrey. Initially, I had wanted to be able to talk to her about my mother, but now I just wanted to see her before there came a time when I no longer could. Unfortunately for Audrey, that time would come sooner than expected.

I made a plan to go see Lesley and Audrey the following week. Lesley put me in touch with two women who had also grown up in Westchester—Judy and Sheri. Coincidentally, both of these women were available the same day I picked. Judy used to date one of my mom's cousins, Harvey, in high school. She and I chatted on the phone, gabbing about both of my "uncles": Lucky, my mom's stepbrother, and Harvey. I was surprised at how Judy spoke of them, as I could not see them having been "cool guys" in high school.

We were a dynamic bunch that day in Orange County, gathering to go into Audrey's board-and-care. As I looked around the facility, which appeared to be more like a house turned hotel, I thought of how Audrey had brought us all together.

After we all did our initial greetings, our gazes fell collectively back to her. Four women were standing there, admiring the lady they loved. Audrey did not look the same, however. Lesley had not been kidding—Audrey could not get up or speak. She could barely blink. She had been sleeping when we got there and was all snuggled up in her twin bed in white sheets. She was stripped down to the bare minimum: pajamas, instead of a yellow suit; hearing aids, instead of elaborate broaches and earrings. A beige blanket, instead of a beige pashmina from one of her trips to Milan. Much to my surprise, given the rest of her transformation, her hair was still up in a high French twist. I pondered whether it could have stayed that perfect since 1999, the last time I had seen her.

I wanted to sit and gossip with her and talk about how much we both missed my mom. I wanted her to tell me about

Ethel and ask her what her opinion was of my family in the 1950s. I wanted her to tell me she liked my hair color. I wanted to know so many things, but all I could hope to get from Audrey today was for her eyes to open, instead of her usual wink and smile. It was tough to see Audrey frail and weak, but she was one of those people who are able to create their own space in your heart. And for the time being, it was enough just to be in her presence, whether she was coherent or not.

"Wake up, Audrey!" Sheri yelled, shaking the bed to get her attention. "Come on, party girl," Judy shouted. They did a good job to lighten the mood, as I was on the verge of tears. I hated seeing Audrey in this state, but this also would mean that soon there would be one fewer person in the world who was close to my mom. I went to Audrey's side and rubbed her chapped face, wishing I had some of my Kate Somerville lotion to put on it. "Audrey, it's me, Jessica Barraco. Remember me? Remember my mother, Dianne?"

Between my rubbing her face and Sheri's shaking the bed, we managed to awaken Audrey enough that her eyes opened slightly. This would be the first of many breakthroughs Sheri and I would make together. A new team was forming—a theme song should have been playing—and we did not even know it. Audrey looked surprised at her own eyelids' ability to move. She stared at me and opened her mouth to speak, but nothing came out.

"Mommy, it's me," Lesley shouted suddenly. Audrey moved her neck about two degrees in Lesley's direction, then stopped; she could go no more. *Come on, Audrey,* I kept cheering for her in my head. Then her head went back down and her eyes closed. That was all we would get for the day.

Afterward, all of us chatted, happy that we had almost gotten Audrey to speak. We'd never thought there would come a time when we wouldn't be able to hear Audrey's voice. They wanted to know how I knew Audrey, how exactly I was related to Lucky, and why I was doing all of this research. Sitting at Mimi's Café, eating blueberry muffins and salad, I had made two new "aunts" and had been introduced to more help and information than I knew would be necessary.

One lady they knew had dated my uncle Monte, who was beloved by so many but who had tragically passed away of AIDS in 1991. For five hours, they gossiped and gabbed as if they had graduated high school yesterday. They spoke of people I knew and people I didn't. They told me their faint memories of my mom, since she was younger than most of them, and their vivid memories of my grandparents Ethel and Jack. From their recollections, I was able to dig into 1964, take a seat, and witness the action happening then. Bill Mercer was my mother's childhood love—he went to Vietnam. I presumed he had died there but couldn't be sure of anything at this point. The ladies did not know Bill but were curious to learn about him. That we were separating fact from fiction is an understatement.

IT WAS A RAINY DAY WHEN I got the call from Lesley a few months later. I was exhausted. My grandma had just turned ninety-one, and she had received a pacemaker for her birthday. Seeing her go through a weeklong stay at the hospital, as well as a grueling surgery for a device that would literally send electric shocks to her heart to make it beat faster every second of the day, had been too much for me to handle. The whole week, I had been trying to tell myself to be strong but had ended up spending ten hours a day in the hospital with her. Sheer adrenaline kept me from crying every minute.

Grandma was funny in the hospital when I went to visit her, though. She definitely had a storytelling gene and wouldn't let the hospital slow her down. She told my best friend and me all about how her husband had died in Miami Beach. After they had "sexual relations, you know," he passed out, and by the time the ambulance came, Benny Barraco was dead.

"I killed him," Grandma said to me, with unusually wide eyes.

"Grandma, no, you didn't! He probably had a brain aneurism."

"Yeah, yeah. Whatevah," she said in her heavy New York accent. Grandma's ability not to give a shit about things that most people have heart attacks over is why she lived for ninety-three years.

I had just returned from the hospital when I answered the phone to hear Lesley's voice. "Audrey passed away last Sunday, October 10; 10/10/10 is now a special day," she said. My heart sank. While I had been tending to one grandma in the hospital, another grandma had left the earth.

Later that week, I attended Audrey's funeral. Only a handful of people showed up for the party girl. I was mentioned in the eulogy that the rabbi made, and he sang a beautiful poem that my cantor sings during regular *yizkor* memorial services. I was sure Audrey had heard it before.

As I tossed three shovels of dirt on her grave and wiped my

hands on my black dress, I looked down. My shoes matched my
bag, and I was wearing my grandmother's cameo as a brooch.
How appropriate. I looked up and saw my mom. She was
smiling at me, smiling at Audrey's memory. I blinked, and the
clouds shifted northwest. I could have sworn I heard Audrey
and Di whispering in heaven, but it might have been just a gust
of Santa Ana winds.

A t just fourteen, Dianne was quite the sight to see. Getting ready for school in the morning took some time, even though she had showered and laid out her clothes the night before. Having recently bleached her dark brown hair to turn it a sunny red color, Dianne was obsessed with keeping up the vitality of each strand. Spraying Aqua Net all over her curls kept them in place yet bouncy for the rest of the school day. Turning up the radio dial to hear her new favorite song, "He's So Fine," she sang along loudly. Dianne was not like most girls, though, and she snickered to herself as she put on her blue knee socks.

She had a date later that evening with Bill Mercer. *Should I go all the way with him tonight?* she wondered, teasing her auburn curls for more volume. Grasping her blue wide-toothed comb from her vanity drawer, she heard a knock at the door. "Little Leslie, time for breakfast!"

"I'm not Leslie; I'm Dianne!" she shouted. "And I'm still doing my hair! I'm not hungry. Eat without me."

In came her stepbrother, Lucky, who could not decipher a boundary if the letters were spelled out in front of him. "Ugh, can't you knock?" Dianne asked, with her usual aggravated tone.

"I did knock—I told you it was breakfast time. Hey, who are you going out with tonight, Little Sis?"

"I'm not your sister! We aren't even blood related." Picking up her brown leather schoolbag, Dianne rushed out of her room, bed unmade. *Evelyn will do it later*, she thought.

Walking into the light and airy Westchester kitchen of Jack and Ethel, Dianne gazed adoringly at her stepfather, Jack, who she wished was her biological father. "Good morning, Dad! Anything interesting in the paper today?"

Jack showed her the front of the *Los Angeles Times*. "Looks like we're sending some troops to Vietnam soon, my darling. Such a shame, such a shame."

"Now, Jack, let's not repeat negative news so early in the morning." Ethel shook her hands on her apron. "Leslie, want to break the eggshells for me?"

"Sure, Mommy." Dianne allowed her mother to call her Leslie, her birth name, because she figured her mother had earned the right to; she *had* carried her around in her belly for nine months, after all, Dianne thought.

Dianne was born Leslie Dianne Spungin on April 3, 1950. Never a fan of her birthday, she focused on one thing: her birthstone—a diamond. How she dreamed of having a big diamond on her left ring finger one day, one that was much larger than the ring her mother had. Jack did just fine, but Ethel had learned years before that being married to a successful doctor with plenty of money (her first husband, Sy) was no substitute for love. Jack loved her, and Jack loved her daughter, and that was worth more than any diamond in the world.

"Pancakes or waffles?" Ethel asked with a smile on her face. Her green, sweetheart-neckline dress with a pink-and-red-plaid apron over it emitted the essence of a wonderful 1950s housewife. The beauty that rested deep in her eyes, however, masked the vanity of an aspiring actress—a dream she would never achieve, even though her hair always looked camera-ready.

"Pancakes!" Lucky shouted as he ran into the room, belt undone, shirt unbuttoned, revealing his pudgy belly. At times, he resembled a fifty-year-old man more than a seventeen-year-old boy.

Dianne finished cracking the eggs and watched the yoke explode out of its casing, wondering if it was sufficiently matured—whatever that meant. Sometimes she worried that a baby chicken would still be inside one of these shells, as a girl at school had told her the year before. She shuddered at the thought. "Mommy! I left some pieces of shell in the bowl," Dianne said, distracted and troubled.

"Don't worry about it, sweetheart; it's nothing a spoon or a fork can't fix." Ethel scooped away the pieces of shell and mixed the eggs in with the rest of the pancake batter. Dianne poured Jack and Lucky coffee from the yellow KitchenAid coffeemaker, which she had always liked. *Kitchens should always be yellow*, she thought.

"Pancakes it is," Ethel exclaimed. "Leslie, will you hand me the spatula, please?" As Dianne opened the left-hand drawer, the memory came flooding back to her. Ethel and her father, Sy, had divorced in 1955 and had fought more than any two people should during the events that led up to their split. Dianne had witnessed their nastiest fight when she was only five years old. Running into the house after ballet class, wearing a pink leotard and matching ballet shoes, she heard her parents yelling. The mother of her best friend, Donna, had driven her home that day, as she had during much of Dianne's early childhood. Other people's parents often drove her home during the divorce.

Dianne's parents were in the kitchen; the walls were a pale yellow. "Don't you ever speak that way to me, woman!" Sy screamed.

"I know what you did!" Ethel screamed back. "I know what you did with that nurse at the hospital—everyone knows!" Ethel had been cleaning the dishes in the sink and stopped to sob against the refrigerator. Young Dianne watched from the entryway of the house as her father slapped her mother across the face with a spatula. Sy ran into his office. Both Ethel and Dianne threw their hands up to their faces and cried.

Dianne rushed into the kitchen to see if her mother was all right. "Mommy? Are you okay? Why did Daddy do that?"

"Yes, I'll be fine, honey. But we need to talk for a minute."

It was then that Ethel broke the news to Dianne that she was going to divorce her ballistic doctor of a father who was cheating on her whenever he got a coffee break at the hospital. The audacity he had, she vented to her five-year-old: "You know Mommy practically paid his way through school."

Dianne nodded, too young to know about money troubles and much too young to have seen what she had just witnessed. The memory was irreversible.

"HERE'S THE SPATULA, MOMMY." Dianne handed the utensil to her mother, her hands cold and shaky from the flashback. Maybe she could catch the early bus to Westchester High School, she thought. Quickly, Dianne tried to focus on her upcoming drive-in date with Bill for later that evening. Her morning had not gotten off to a great start.

When she finally arrived at school, Dianne rushed up the stairs. She had spent way too much extra time teasing her hair. Dianne had a sister, twelve years Dianne's senior, and was already married with children. Dianne often reflected on what a nice relationship the two sisters could have had—"could" being the operative word.

Jumping up the stairs to get to her locker, Dianne was confronted by Lesley, a girl in her grade. She was one of the few Jewish people at her school and was the daughter of Audrey Neller, a neighbor of Jack and Ethel's. "Hi, Leslie," said Lesley. "How are you doing this morning?"

"It's Dianne, Lesley—I'm going by my middle name, remember?"

"Oh, that's right—gee, I don't know why you don't like your real name, Dianne. We could be name twins!"

"Right," said Dianne. "I've got to get to Geometry. Nice seeing you." Lesley meant well, but the two Leslies would never become close. Lesley's mother, Audrey, however, was a personal favorite of Dianne's. Dianne could not have known it then, but she and Audrey would be great friends much later in life. Lesley went to Jewish camp in the summers and led a clean lifestyle. Dianne had had her first alcoholic drink at age eleven. By now, she was a whiskey straight shooter and could keep up with her eighteen-year-old boyfriend, Bill, and his friends.

Geometry and the rest of the day went by slowly, as Dianne doodled "Dianne Mercer" on each and every one of her boring black academic notebooks. On one of the pages she saw, "You stink!" written in by who else but Lucky. Dianne smirked as she thought of the strange relationship she and Lucky had. Because they were close in age and step-siblings, Lucky was protective of her but sometimes had an odd way of showing it.

She shook her head and focused on Bill. *Oh, Bill.*

Bill was like the Prince Charming of her town. He was an all-star. During his time at Westchester High School, he was the president and founder of his surf club, ran track, and always had a smile plastered on his corn-fed face. His parents hailed from Nebraska and Colorado, so Bill had the looks of a Scot. With strawberry-blond hair and a freckle-specked face, he may not have been classically handsome, yet he still managed to be the big man on campus. In Westchester in the early 1960s, you were into hot rods, surfing, or academics. Only two of those were cool, as you can imagine, and Bill had a black low-rider car, and surfing accolades to boot. All of the teachers loved him and enjoyed having him in class. His goals in life were to be a good husband and father, raise a family in San Diego so he could surf every day, and go to medical school.

He was going to be something special, this Dianne knew. Growing up in a family of two boys and kind parents, Bill had the perfect home life, which intimidated Dianne at times. He was so *Leave It to Beaver*, and Dianne's home was anything but that. For this reason, she did not wish to be around the Mercers very often. She had always pictured herself wanting to get to know her first boyfriend's family well, but the Mercers intimidated her so much that she thought there was no way they would accept a girl who did not come from perfection. The distance Dianne kept to protect herself would cause her trouble in the future, but at the time, she believed it was her prerogative to be around, or not. She was only fourteen, for goodness sake!

Dianne felt ashamed for being a product of divorce. She couldn't help but wonder if she was the reason her parents separated; they seemed to have been happy when they had only one child, her older sister. Dianne did not miss the times she heard her parents fighting to no end until the early-morning hours, when Dianne was already tucked into her bed and squeezing two pillows over her ears, trying to drown out her mother's cries.

Jack was not a rich man, but he was a kind one. He was a member of the Dirty Jokes Club, a club that married men joined to have a few drinks and tell mildly inappropriate jokes to one another once a month. The only baggage he carried with him was his son. Dianne would find a lifelong friend in her annoying stepsibling, so the sands did turn eventually, but not for nearly a decade.

Always looking the part of the First Lady, Ethel loved to go out and tried to pursue acting, singing, and dancing whenever possible. While Dianne was at school at a young age and Ethel was trying to work out her feelings about the divorce, she would go to the beauty parlor with her sister, Florence, who lived down the street. There, the women would sit under light green and yellow–tinted heat lamps as their bouffants and dye jobs settled into their individual locks. Having grown up as close sisters in New York City, Ethel and Florence had a falling-out in 1962; however, they remained quite close during Ethel's divorce. This proved to be a rough yet fascinating time in

Ethel's life. She regretted not having become an actress, as that was one of many motivations to relocate from New York City to California.

The story goes that she had met Sy when he was a dashing young waiter in the Catskills and decided to follow his medical school dream as she chased the stage. Oh, how she would have loved to star on Broadway, and as an elderly woman in *Knots Landing*. Instead, she worked for a real estate mogul who helped pay her and Sy's rent when they were a young married couple, as well as helped Sy get into (and footed the bill for) USC medical school. The two lovebirds were thrilled. Sy had worked every summer night and day to put himself through college, so to have a free ride for medical school was a dream come true. However, it was not a free ride. Ethel would become the mogul's twenty-four-hour personal assistant and secretary for eight years. It was hard work for a girl who had meant to become a professional performer, not a typist. But she was in love, and if Ethel was in love, like her daughter, she would do absolutely anything for that person. Aside from her charm and beauty, Ethel passed another thing along to her daughter—loving men who did not deserve her.

Back in the last period of school, Dianne twirled her strawberry-blond hair and drummed her red fingernails on the table, waiting with bated breath for Bill's appearance on the bleachers that afternoon.

*J*ake, get away from the overpass!"

"Relax; it's fine. I'm just waving at the people who pass by."

"We came here to go to the beach, not the freeway. Come on!" I screamed, this time successfully tugging at the white undershirt he wore as a T-shirt and handing him the big bag of Cheetos we had bought from the corner convenience store to take to the beach. It was my twentieth birthday. He pulled me close, with Cheetos still in his mouth, and said, "Why do you worry so much?"

Do you have any idea how many times I have been asked that question in my life? I like to think of myself as super-cautious, rather than as a terminal worrywart. I take life seriously, I guess. I can feel the gravity of our days being numbered, and I respect life too much to stick a limb out over a freeway overpass. But could I articulate this to my twenty-three-year-old boyfriend? Not a chance. All I could do was show him how much I loved him by worrying, and of course by having constant sex to cover all the holes in our relationship. If our relationship had been a sweater and a homeless person had seen it on the floor, even he would have passed it up in the dead of winter. But drama was comfortable to me. At least it wasn't a life-or-death situation.

Jake still looked concerned, but not for my emotions; rather, he seemed to be calculating in his head how blatantly different we were. How many more mental tallies did I have until the inevitable breakup? "I'm not being dramatic, I promise. My uncle knew someone who committed suicide right here, and it just . . . just makes me uncomfortable, that's all."

"All right, baby, all right." We went along the overpass, walking hand in hand.

I was wearing a white bikini that day, and Jake took my picture. I looked across the water, out into the ocean, and saw a rock with two seals on it. *Lovebirds*, I thought. Would Jake be my mate always? And then it hit me. Could I really fall in love—forever—this young? Whatever happened to Bill Mercer, the boy my mom used to talk about whenever we sat at the beach on family trips? Did she love him forever? I pictured her looking similar to me in my white bikini, hair up in a Gidget bun, wearing cat-eyed sunglasses, instead of aviators, watching Bill surf. He'd died, hadn't he? I wasn't so sure at that moment. Jake was occupied on his phone—the latest version of the Black-Berry had just come out—and I glared up into the sun, getting lost in the light. I saw myself at four years old in Washington, DC, with my family.

At the Vietnam Memorial, the lines of graves were positively haunting, and I remember, even at four, wondering why my mom had not let my sister and me stay in the hotel room while my parents went on this not-so-uplifting journey into their generation's past.

"I had a college roommate who was drafted," said my father, by way of explanation, his sad brown eyes glancing around the cemetery. My mom said nothing; she appeared to be in a trance. Her green eyes fixed an invisible hex on the large, fine-print book of fallen soldiers.

Hands in my pockets, I sat down, as I did not feel like traipsing around in the cold. I was notorious for being lazy on family trips as a toddler. Everyone thought this one video of me as a child at Disney World was hilarious. In it, I was upset to be walking in the semicold weather; I kept a foot's distance behind the rest of my family, wearing a too-big-for-my-body poncho. But this time, I watched my mother closely as she approached the book and started leafing through every feather-thin piece of paper. Each page had at least two hundred names on it.

"Can we help you," a stranger asked her.

"No, thanks," she said as she shook her head. Tossing her short hair with her polished red fingernails, she calmly skimmed the pages, as if she were delicately rubbing a baby's cheeks.

All of a sudden, a strong gust of wind blew over the memorial, and I stood up. We all heard my mother gasp and hold her gloved hand to the page, staring in disbelief. "Jess, come over here," she said. I scurried over to my mother's side. "This was my first boyfriend, Bill Mercer. He died in 1965, defending his country."

"How'd you find his name, Mommy?" I asked. At that time, I couldn't even read, so whittling down the thousands of names behooved me. My entire family had crowded around us, but I got the impression that she wanted only me around. She wanted us to be in the walk-in closet again. "The wind showed it to me," she said, with tears in her eyes.

"JESSICA!" Jake had been tapping me for a few minutes, vigilantly shaking me out of my daydream. "It's getting cold. Can we go back to the hotel now?" I looked over at him, tears in my eyes, which my aviator sunglasses were covering, and nodded. I got up to wipe the sand off my legs and looked around.

I made a promise to myself that day: before I had my own wedding and before I found the right person to marry, I would find out Bill's fate. Had my mother even known?

"No more worrying today," Jake said. "Let's get a bottle of wine and get drunk tonight," he said, a boyish gleam in his eyes. Even though he was saying the words, I couldn't quite process them. Perhaps, as with so many things in my life, something about our relationship fed my worrisome soul instead of comforting it. Something in his look told me: *this isn't forever*. I tried to shake off my fear and took his hand as we exited the sandy beach.

I do my best thinking on the beach. So did my mom. Her thoughts unfolded as inconsistently and all-consumingly as the waves crashed down on the shore. Taking my last step off the sandy stairs, I saw a butterfly in the distance. I blinked, and it was gone.

When Jake and I broke up six months later, I thought of that moment on the beach, and I thought of Bill. It was almost as if my life was etched in stone already, marked by my mother's relationships. Jake always reminded me of Bill—they were both our first loves. They were both responsible for our very first heartbreaks, and all our firsts. But he was gone. We parted ways on a snowy Valentine's Day in Denver.

It became my duty to find out what Bill was responsible for in my mother's life. There might have been a blizzard outside, but it was my heart that had frozen over. My present circumstance was always finding a way to steal my curiosity of my mother's past away from me. The white water of wonder washed over me and receded quickly, uncovering tiny holes that the sand crabs had taken thirty precious seconds to make. There were too many inconceivable holes in my life to be uncovering hers right then, though, and not enough butterflies.

DIANNE

1964

*C*hasing each other into the bathroom, Donna, Dianne's best friend, and Dianne took a long glance at themselves in the mirror. Donna was dating Jerry, a very handsome boy on the diving team. He was in Bill's grade, so the four of them hung out as often as they could. They went out in Hollywood sometimes, to the eighteen-and-over clubs. Donna and Dianne knew how to primp themselves to look older than fourteen, so they usually had no trouble getting into the clubs. It was there that Dianne discovered that she was more suited for partner dancing than for one-on-one lessons. Although she did take ballet and lyrical jazz classes at Cyd Charisse's dance studio on Third Street in West Hollywood, she much preferred being hip to hip with Bill at the Revelaire Club.

When Ethel drove her to dance class, they always stopped at the Apple Pan for a quick dinner, or a piece of apple pie if it wasn't dinnertime. Ethel never ate the French fries but let Dianne order some. Dianne always ended up slipping the owner a few fries when no one was looking.

"I bet the burgers aren't half as good as the Apple Pan's,"

Dianne said to Donna, pouting at the mirrored image of the half bun, half ponytail she had thrown her hair up in.

"Too Gidget," Donna said with a flat smirk.

"You're right," Dianne muttered. "I hate when you're right because I'm having a flat-hair day!"

"I've been having a flat-hair year," Donna exclaimed, and the two girls went on laughing. They always had so much fun together talking about nothing too much—it was how they had found common ground. Donna's home life was not stable, either. As a psychologist would say, like attracts like.

"Pink sweater or red sweater?" Dianne asked, a confused look in her eye.

"Red, D; for sure, red! Tonight is the night, and red is the color of passion."

Dianne rolled her eyes. Donna sure was a pervert sometimes. "Hand me the rouge," Dianne ordered.

"Not done with it yet," Donna yelled into the bathroom mirror. Dianne went into the stall.

"Say, who wrote their initials on the bathroom stall? 'J and H'?"

"Hello, Dianne . . . probably Harvey and some girl?"

"I should have known," Dianne said, as she scribbled "D&B" in small, inconspicuous print with red lipstick.

"Did you know Jerry gave me his letters the other day," asked Donna.

"When Bill goes to college next year, maybe he'll give me his fraternity pin! It's four o'clock, Don—gotta go! Wish me luck!"

"Good luck, D," Donna said, with a wink and a pat on the butt.

Wearing a red-and-blue-striped dress, her hair down from

the high Gidget bun and turned into a mini-bouffant, Dianne took a few deep breaths. She and Bill had been seeing each other for over a year, and while Dianne was no prude, she had never had sex before. She wanted Bill to be the one who changed her world as she knew it. Sometimes it was so hard getting attention at home. Ethel was busy playing her perfect-housewife role, and Jack was always at work or the temple.

Dianne needed someone for herself, and only her. She was certain that if she could find someone who cared only about her, he would be the right person for her, and she thought that might be Bill. Still, she enjoyed the "fun in the sun" kind of relationship they had, too, even if it involved sometimes sharing Bill with his friends, whom she was not fond of. They were nice guys, with Beaver Cleaver–type home lives, and Dianne did not feel comfortable spending time with them. Their lives seemed so much simpler than hers.

As the cool night air rose from the nearby Pacific, Dianne wrapped her red sweater around her shoulders. Bill had not been in school that day because he was taking tests for the draft. Dianne was frightened at the possibility of his leaving, but she had plenty of uncles and brothers of friends who had been drafted in previous wars, and they had come out all right. It was part of life then, and Dianne could not focus on the negative, even though Bill was her only positive. She was not even sure he would go to Vietnam, as he wanted to attend medical school, and usually the boys who made good grades and were accepted to a university right away were able to skip the draft. Dianne shuddered and thanked God quickly that they did not draft women. She would be the worst soldier; she'd just bitch everyone out and ask for a cigarette. She smiled satirically at that image.

Sitting on the wooden bleachers, with her hands tucked behind her knees, she waited. And waited, and waited. Where was Bill? Were his tests over? Was he stuck at the doctor's? Had he gotten into an accident? An hour went by, and Dianne started to get worried. She decided she would stop by his house and ask his mother, Maple, where he might be. Bill was not the type to stand Dianne up. He was reliable and strong.

Just as she was collecting her schoolbag, someone tapped her on the shoulder. Her green eyes widened as she saw Bill standing there with a big white envelope in his hand. He looked undeniably sad; Dianne could read his facial expression. "Bill? What is it? What's the matter?"

"I'm going to the war, cute girl. I have to start training and boot camp this summer."

Dianne's heart sank. They wouldn't even get one more summer together. "But I thought you could get out of it since you're applying to college."

"I did, too, but I just found out I can be a medic in Vietnam, and I get to pick my military department." A chill shot through Dianne, as her father had been a medic in World War II. Bill went on, "I'm choosing the Navy because it should be the safest for this war. I'll be either on a ship or on high ground, away from most combat. The Navy isn't even drafting; they barely need me. Plus, I should be gone for only a year at the most. I'll just . . . I'll just . . ." Bill started to tear up.

"You'll what?" Dianne asked, the emotions rising up in her throat as well.

"I'll just miss you." Bill embraced her. "I've been thinking about tonight for a while."

"So have I," she replied.

"Let's go to the drive-in. They're playing *Casablanca*."

"There's nowhere else I'd rather be," Dianne replied. Bill picked up her schoolbag and took her hand. She walked with Bill into the distance, solemnly and slowly but also full of teenage hope and happy to be with him in the moment.

When they arrived at the Centinela Drive-In, Bill set out a blanket and put down the backseat in his blue T-Bird. He had even taken his orange-and-white surfboard off the roof of his car for the night's events. Neither of them was hungry. It was not a popular evening out at the drive-in, as it was a school night. Bill's parents let him have free rein because he was eighteen years old, and Ethel had let Dianne stay out late for a date, which was one of the very groovy things about her antimothering personality.

The credits opened. Rick's Café Américain appeared on the screen as Humphrey Bogart saw Ingrid Bergman for the first time. Dianne laughed and thought how the actors had probably seen each other a million times but Bogart made it look so special, so hopeful, and so romantic. Bill grabbed Dianne's hand as they cuddled and waited for Dianne's favorite part, to which Bill mouthed along with Bogart, "Here's lookin' at you, kid."

Bill handed her a flask with some whiskey in it, and she took a swig and felt the warm alcohol course through her body. Maybe it was the afternoon's news, maybe it was the night air, maybe it was the movie, but something in Dianne shifted. She looked at him with her intense green eyes and grabbed his face quite ferociously. They were hungry for each other, and Dianne saw that she truly loved Bill. Her red ribbon coiled on the floor of the car. Bill pulled the top up as the movie continued to play.

Elsa couldn't make up her mind in *Casablanca*, but Dianne

did at the drive-in. Bill was going to be the one she lost her virginity to, and it was going to be romantic. He was struggling with her dress buttons. Dianne took charge. She straddled Bill and undid the buttons herself, then lifted her dress up over her head to reveal her lacy blue bra and knickers. Bill kissed her all over and told her again and again, "You are so beautiful, you are so beautiful." They kissed until their mouths were red and nearly raw. Dianne could feel the bulge rising up in Bill's pants as she undid his fitted jeans. Bill had one packet of protection. Dianne thought, *I wish there was a condom for my heart.* Her mind raced, until all of a sudden, Bill was inside her and she felt the earth move slightly. Bill pinched her at first, and then she held on to him and tried to enjoy the ride. She had never felt so bonded to someone in her whole life. She knew that this definitely meant Bill was the one. Dianne Mercer was who she would be in the future, and she would just have to wait until after the war to become her.

Bill cried out a few minutes later, as Dianne was interrupted by an explosion of her own. Butterflies floated up through her body as she felt a heat wave and tingling shivers all at the same time.

"Bill . . . ," she whispered. She looked him straight in the eye and said, "I love you."

Bill smiled and held her tight. "I love you, Dianne Spungin. Will you wait for me while I'm away?"

Dianne nodded. They made love once more before Bergman stepped onto the plane headed back to America. But Bogart and Dianne were both destined to be left behind.

B lowing out my twenty-three birthday candles, I thought of two men. Ex-boyfriends? Past love affairs? Nope. I had never even met, much less been involved with, either of the men I was thinking of: Frank Parker and Bill Mercer. Although I was surrounded by smiling friends, great Italian food, twinkly lights, and a date, I always said, "I am chronically single on my birthday." In reality, I haven't spent a birthday alone since I was eighteen years old. My friends could attest to this, but you could have fooled me. The truth was, I never felt "with" these guys. I just sort of walked alongside them. It's easy not to sleep alone, physically. The great feat is not to feel lonely while you're sharing the bed.

I looked around the glimmering table. Something had to give. I thought voices were singing me the "Happy Birthday" song. I hated the "and many more" part. It seemed like I should have been knocking on wood when people said that. I closed my eyes, took a deep breath, stared down at my polka-dot dress with one eye open, closed them again, nervously adjusted my hair away from my eyebrow, and blew out the candles. I exhaled and muttered to nobody, "Where are they, Mom? Where are they?"

When I got home, my birthday date gave me a gift. It was wrapped in a paper towel (I'm not kidding). I had told him, very early on, about my mom's favorite song: "Cherry Bomb" by John Mellencamp. He had taken it to heart the way I had. I told him about a very personal moment when I was going through her funeral box, reading eulogies, the guest book, and I was about to lose my shit, and all of a sudden, "Cherry Bomb" came on my iTunes shuffle. It was her. She was there in spirit. I didn't cry one tear of pain—only three or four tears of sentiment.

"Open it up," he said, with a grin on his face. He was cute, even for a nerd. He was not my type, but there was something sweet about him that I couldn't resist. And he wasn't a bad kisser. Plus, I was twenty-three and trying to write a book in a city that did not make it easy for me. I could use all the comfort I could get.

"What is it?" I giggled, opening the makeshift wrapping paper (a few sheets of paper towels). And then there it was, like a bad car accident you can't stop staring at in your rearview mirror. "Cherry Bomb." In my hand. The original record re-cording from 1987—coincidentally, the year I was born. Perhaps my mom listened to it while she was pregnant with me.

"I found it online, and I just had to get it for you."

I had tears in my eyes. He probably had no idea what he had just done for me. I would end up sleeping with him that night, even though I hadn't been planning on it. When I had blown the candles out earlier, I'd had no intention of that person seeing me naked. Frankly, it had been the furthest thing from my mind. But since he'd given me "Cherry Bomb," there had to be more in store. Right?

"This means the world to me," I said, meaning every syllable. I went to the bathroom to collect myself. I felt safe. I felt loved. I felt "Cherry Bomb." Nostalgia filled the air as I combed through my light brown hair. I stared at myself in the mirror for a long time—something I admittedly used to do too much when I was maybe thirteen or fourteen. I think I was in awe of my own body changing. I saw something changing within me in that moment. It wasn't so much my body; it was my spirit. I was becoming a woman somehow. I hadn't been sure I would without my mother. In a way, my wish had come true in less than an hour. Damn, my mom was good. I took off my birthday dress and gazed at my birthday suit. I exhaled and said to nobody, "Where is my 'Cherry Bomb'?"

THE NEXT DAY, I e-mailed Sheri and told her that I wanted her help to search Vietnam records and military profiles for Bill. It occurred to me that I did not know the exact year in which he died, and that information would help me fill in a few more blanks about my mother's timeline. Nearly two hours after I sent Sheri the e-mail, I was grabbing a cup of coffee at Peet's when I got an e-mail from her on my BlackBerry. The subject was "bill?"

I cannot understand how this lady works so quickly, I thought. *She truly is Double o Sheri*, the nickname I invented for her after she found my mother's first marriage certificate in forty-five minutes the same day I met her. I opened the e-mail, my heart beating hard in my chest. *I might be staring at the fate of Bill*

Mercer right now in this coffee shop, I thought, looking around and noticing all of the people going about their day, having no idea that the e-mail I was reading was so significant. My red finger-nails scrolled down as I encountered his military profile.

"Title: Hospital Corpsman." Yes, that would be accurate, as he had been a medic. "Branch of Service: Navy." Also made sense. "William Ivan Mercer. Birth date: December 19, 1946. Tour date start: December 18, 1966." Bill had started his tour the day before his twentieth birthday. My mom must have been so upset she could not throw him a party or spend the day with him. Instead, he got a rifle and emergency surgical tools for his birthday. This had to be Bill. The profile even stipulated his military service number, B980863. Then it hit me like a sucker punch to my stomach. I almost spit out my mouthful of warm coffee. "Death date: Saturday, June 15, 1968." Bill died at just twenty-two years old—nearly my age. The extended profile listed that he had been awarded the Navy Cross by the president of the United States for saving several lives while losing his own.

Legend has it that Bill served as senior corpsman of Company M, Third Battalion, Fourth Marines, on a combat hill in Quang Tri, South Vietnam. While conducting a sector search of the battalion defense perimeter, Company M became heavily engaged with a large North Vietnamese army force, and many casualties ensued. Bill assisted the injured marines and ushered them to a covered area for treatment, ensuring their final movement to the battalion landing zone for thorough medical evacuation. Over the course of nearly one hour, Bill darted to the points of heaviest contact and maneuvered about the fire-swept terrain and rice paddies to treat men who lay wounded in their fighting holes.

After surviving that stressful hour, Bill volunteered to join the platoon that was assigned the mission of searching the area forward for allies. During Bill's accompaniment of that unit, he came under acute enemy sniper fire—commonly known as a firefight. He forged ahead into the firefight. Bill hid in a covered position for a while but dodged through the turmoil to save a fallen marine, maneuvering across the hazardous area to the side of the soldier. Bill shielded the man with his own body as he administered first aid, and then carried the man to a position of relative safety. Bill noticed another soldier lying in a dangerous area exposed to the intense fire, and rushed to his aid, again using his own body to protect the marine from the hostile shots. While administering medical treatment to a second Marine he attempted to bring to safety, Bill was fatally wounded by the North Vietnamese fire. So it ends: "By his daring initiative, exceptional valor, and inspiring actions, he was directly responsible for saving the lives of several wounded men. His selfless devotion to duty was in keeping with the highest traditions of the United States Naval Service."

"Good luck," the Air Force pilot probably said to Bill as he let down the helicopter's ladder, putting Bill in the most extreme line of fire.

"Good luck to those soldiers," Bill might have replied as he rappelled down the ladder into midair, heading for the rice paddies.

"Bill, are you armed?"

"No, sir. I came here to save lives, not take them." Bill saved several soldiers that day, but he would never get to save himself, and he would never get to save my mother.

As I sat down in the chair nearest to me, trying to take in all of these details, everything was crystal clear. Now that I'd learned how Bill had died, saving several soldiers, so much of what my mom had told me suddenly made sense. Bill was supposed to have been the person she would spend the rest of her life with. He was her first love. He was supposed to be a surgeon but ended up dying a war hero too young. He received the honor of the Navy Cross, and although his remains were recovered, Dianne never visited the grave. It was too hard for her. She got in the car many times to drive to the Catholic cemetery in Culver City, but every time she got in the car, I imagine, all she could think of was driving down Anise to turn onto Bill's street and give him a hug. He was buried just a few miles from the very place he was supposed to have reached his full potential as a doctor, husband, brother, and father.

Knowing how abandoned my mom felt by her father, and then by Bill, who was her only foreseeable "hope" of a man treating her correctly, I empathized with her teenage mind, which saw no light at the end of the tunnel. I could psychologically understand her motivations for the next few years of her life and truly wished I could have been there in 1968 to tell her that she would find another man who would love her like Bill did. Or would she?

As I continued to sip my coffee in the same Peet's I had entered no more than ten minutes before, I wondered, *Will I ever find the right guy?* My issues were different from my mother's because I was not afraid of being abandoned, but I shared her fear of wasting time with someone. You entered and left the earth on your own—there was no need to be isolated in the interim. Bill's death was heroic, but it did not matter. I wondered if my mom felt alone that day she heard the news, the same way that I had felt at her funeral. I wondered if she knew on some level that she would also die a hero. The people in the coffeehouse hiding behind their MacBook Pros and Black-Berries would never know the gaping hole that my heart was peeling open to expose. They would never know what it felt like to learn what I had just learned. And they would never know Dianne or Bill. Fresh air seemed like the next-best thing to a shot of bourbon, so I burst through the double glass-paneled doors and somehow went on with my day.

My search to find more information on Bill continued. To hear about people dying too young, and dying while saving their country, is one thing, but to visualize the fight and get to know some of the men who were involved is just way beyond anyone's nightmare. Coming from a generation wherein men are not drafted, I find unfathomable the responsibilities that these young men took on, most just after graduating high school. Vietnam sheds some light on the sociological aspects of war, and why relationships were valued on a different level back then. In my generation's world, we have less at "stake." We can go to school for longer, master advanced degrees, and travel wherever we want. Money is not even the barrier it was before, as there are so many funds for college-age people and financial-aid systems are in place throughout the United States. But for these men, these boys, who went off to war and died there, their lives had to be more significant than the average Joe's. They had more at stake. They had more to lose. It is my firm belief that as evolutionary as it was for men to be non-committal at a young age, these boys grew up faster because the U.S. government left them no choice. The weight of the world was riding on their shoulders, and there was no endpoint in the constant of war—

only a last drop, a vertical plunge into the unknown. Some-times they ended up returning home as heroes; most of the time they ended up dying as heroes. But the lucky ones felt some sort of comfort knowing that some young girl was at home, waiting for them to return. Perhaps that relationship made their probable death seem less plausible.

This thought led me to consider my own high stakes: my research, my writing, the strength to do what I wanted without judgment from others, and getting involved with strangers who might have unresolved issues, but whose memories I relied on to reconstruct my mother's life. I had accepted all of it as my reality, and with the help of several people who just a few months before had been strangers, I had been quite successful and gained a web of insight I never thought I could.

I saw on the military website describing the scene of Bill's death that someone had left a comment. The problem was, the man had commented with an e-mail address that was twelve years old, and the message I sent to him inevitably bounced back. Now I had to go on the hunt for another man: the com-menter. To do this, I needed to call upon my newfound partner in crime—a Westchester gal, Regina. She was fascinated by my investigation for my mom's truths and helped me, quick to the minute, as things unfolded in real time. I quickly explained to her what was going on, and she was on it.

Meeting Regina through a mere interview that I'd thought would be fruitless was the closest I had come so far to striking gold. I had been doing research mostly on my own and had always thought I needed a private detective. In Regina I found one, free of charge. Regina had worked in the Los Angeles Police Department as a detective before women were really on the force. She had to solve homicides without the help of the Internet, and since she had retired and was hooked up to Wi-Fi, she thought research was easy as pie.

The comment read:

I served in Vietnam with the Third Battalion, Fourth Marines, from November of 1968 to June 15, 1969. I was wounded and evacuated out of country that day. My very best friend, William Ivan "Doc" Mercer, was killed in action later that same day. Doc was a corpsman attached to our company. I've wanted to visit Doc's grave and possibly meet his family, I've just never been able to locate much information until today on this site. Thank you, Doc, for getting me out alive. I think of you often and especially on Veterans' Day. I'll never forget you, and I'll look forward to seeing you again.

Within a few hours, Regina found the coordinator contact of the Third Battalion of Company M in the Marine Corps. Matthem, an injured veteran, lived somewhere in the Midwest, and I sent him a handwritten letter in the mail to generate the beginning of a correspondence between us, since no e-mail or phone number had been listed for him online. I sent the letter first class so that it would reach him as soon as possible. Having not sent a letter to a stranger, let's see, ever, I did not expect a response. I spoke to tons of men who were fully aware of my phone number and consciously didn't use it, so I was skeptical that a perfect stranger would pick up the phone and call me back.

You can imagine my surprise when I received a call from Matthew just three days later. I was thrilled! I called him back, and we spoke for a little while. He did not remember Bill, or Doc, but sent out a posting to the Third Battalion military e-mail LISTSERV to see who might.

A few days later, I received an e-mail from a man named Brian Murphy. Murphy was the brother of the Marine, Dick Murphy, who Bill died trying to resuscitate in the firefight. Brian was only ten years old when his brother was killed in the war. For the previous forty years, he had kept up his brother's legacy of protecting others, by rising through the ranks of the Norwood Police Department. He had made it his personal business to keep up with the Vietnam veterans and attend all of the reunions and events to commemorate his big brother, whom, sadly, he would never know as a grown man.

Murphy was delighted to speak with me, and told me that he had been in touch with Bill's brother and mother in the past. My eyes lit up. I knew somehow intuitively that Bill had had a brother, but I didn't know his name. In the way I imagined my mother's relationship with Bill to go, I assumed Bill's brother was named Ivan, Bill's middle name; it just came to me intuitively. Some would call it using your third eye, or perhaps my mom really did enter my subconscious and gave me little hints. To my utter astonishment, Murphy e-mailed me back and said the following:

Jessica,

Attached are photos that Van (Ivan) Mercer sent to me when we first made contact on Memorial Day in 2007. I just sent

him an e-mail about you and your search. I hope he decides
to correspond with you. I am on Facebook as Brian P.
Murphy. Interesting that both Van Mercer and I have our
brother's middle names as our first names. Bill Mercer's
middle name was Ivan, which is Van's given name. Dick's
middle name was Brian.

My eyes widened. How in the hell had I known that Bill's
brother was named Ivan? William and Ivan must have been two
very important people in the Mercers' lives, and I had known
that on some spiritual level. It was then that I experienced one
of those profound moments where I could feel my mom with
me and realized that she was very much a part of my daily
experiences with research and writing, especially regarding Bill.
Although I grew up an inquisitive girl, I'm sure my mother had
no idea that I would be up late researching her first love fifty
years after the fact. I felt a connection to Bill, and I always had,
and I was just following that connection. Unlike my dating
experiences, and to my pleasant surprise, the Mercer connection was not one-sided. And it would progress rapidly.

I should have assumed the military veterans would not be
anything short of efficient. I envisioned that before they
answered my e-mails each morning, they tidied up their rooms,
placing their T-shirts and underwear in carefully color-
coordinated stacks, like a scene out of *A Few Good Men*.
However, I was not expecting such speedy assistance. It was the
night before Thanksgiving, and I was at my weekly wine-club
meeting. The group was called "The Young Winos of LA."
That night the club was tasting a popular Thanksgiving Beau-

jolais that is best paired with turkey, and I was having a great time. The Winos were a group that had helped me acclimate to postcollege life in LA. I made a lot of new friends and even squeezed a few dates out of the group. People got really excited about setting me up, but there was always a catch. In the Young Winos' case, this catch was that the guy already had a girlfriend. Oops. Anyway, while the cheese was being served, I went to check my phone for messages, and that's when I saw it.

One new e-mail. Subject: "Ivan 'Van' Mercer, Bill's brother." My eyes widened, my heart stopped for a second, and my hands started to shake while I sweated profusely. I had found Ivan! I had never in a million years thought I could track him down. Scrolling down, skimming the e-mail, and barely believing my own eyes while crouched in a corner at some random person's apartment, I screamed. All eyes turned to me.

"I did it, I did it, I did it!" I kept saying. I looked at my only friend in the room who knew what was going on, and she said, "What is it?"

"It's Bill's brother!"

"Bill?" she exclaimed. "Oh my god! Bill's brother! That's unbelievable, Jess."

I had to go to the bathroom to collect myself. I just stared in the mirror for a long time, thoughts racing through my head. I had done the impossible; this was what my journey was all about. Finally! Success.

The body of the e-mail contained a timely love story—one that I had first envisioned on my own and then brought to life on the page, just to be confirmed several months later. Most of my intuition had been right. The next few paragraphs informed my story and changed my life.

Jessica,

I am Ivan "Van" Mercer, younger brother of Bill. I remember your mom well. She went by Dianne Taylor, although everyone knew that her real name was Leslie Spungin. I am so sorry to hear of her passing. She and Bill had a very intense relationship that lasted for several years. Before Bill met your mom, he was the founder and president of our surf club, Pacific Shores Surf Club, based in Playa del Rey, and he was the best surfer. After falling in love with your mom, he stopped surfing and stopped hanging around with his friends. He spent all of his time with Dianne. His friends resented Dianne for this, and Bill got into many fights defending her. I hate to admit to this to you, but I was also jealous. Bill was not only my special big brother, but also my best friend. We became strangers to each other for a while. Their relationship could be called an outlaw relationship, as not only friends but both parents were against it. My parents were mad at her for taking Bill's car for a joyride with her friends while Bill was at work at a restaurant. My parents saw her driving their 1956 Ford station wagon and pulled her over. She was too young to have a driver's license at the time. They were nomads, and that was a big part of the romance.

One Christmas holiday season, your mom worked as a gift wrapper at the Broadway in Westchester. The interesting thing is that your grandma paid the store to employ her. She paid her salary. My ninety-year-old mom in Las Vegas brought that fact up in our telephone conversation last week. My mom said that even though she didn't approve of the relationship, she now sees how much they loved each other.

I do not know what ended their relationship. Bill never talked about it. Afterward, I was the matchmaker who introduced Bill to his future wife, Trish. Trish surfed at Playa del Rey, and Bill was getting back into surfing. Even after they were engaged, I know that Bill was sneaking out to see your mom. Trish represented the healthy relationship, and Dianne represented the dark, sexy, and mysterious relationship, that Bill was torn between. Bill, as you have learned some details, left Vietnam for a five-day R&R and met Trish in Hawaii, where they were married. Trish's mom was in the adjacent suite on their wedding night, and she was screaming and breaking things all night. She ended up spending the wedding night with her mother. Bill flew back to Vietnam the next day without consummating the marriage. He was killed one month later.

A few things of his were sent back with his body from Vietnam. In his wallet, there was his 1964 prom picture, from when he took your mom to his senior prom at Westchester High. This picture was one of the last things he ever looked at from home. It is attached.

There was a knock at the door. I had forgotten I was in someone's bathroom, gripping the off-white sink, as I was frozen in time, staring at my BlackBerry. I did not care who was knocking; I had to digest this new information. It was hard enough that I was tipsy on wine I did not even like and would most certainly not drink on Thanksgiving. Bill's mother, at ninety years old, was still upset about how she had handled her son's young relationship with my mother. What? There were so many compelling parts of this story that I could not have premeditated. Better yet, Van wanted to keep in touch with me. He had been looking for my mom, too! And the prom picture—I could not wait for it to download! I wanted to blow it up on my computer and study it for the next week and a half.

I called my sister to tell her the good news. I faced my wino friends, who were looking at me like I was nuts. I *was* sort of nuts, but I would explain it to them. I just needed some cheese on a cracker and some time to contemplate the e-mail.

My mom and Bill: the Romeo and Juliet of Westchester, California. How fascinating. Everyone nodded and smiled at me, not really understanding the blood, sweat, and tears I had put into this new development, but wanting to. I was not sure I could even understand it. Most people do not get the sense of accomplishment and effort that I have from my research until they have a child. I gave birth to information. It consumed me, it lived inside my soul for so long, and then it resurfaced, bringing me closer to my mother from beyond the grave. It was only November of my twenty-fourth year of life, and already one-half of my wish had come true. Would that be good enough for me?

*W*ell, listen, I think we should plan a going-away party for Bill, kind of like a bon voyage thingamajig. How does that sound? We could do it at the house," said Ethel.

Dianne furrowed her eyebrows together first and then raised her left one, to try to control the glare of sheer hatred of Ethel that was forming. "Sure, that's fine; I'd be happy to," Dianne lied through a clenched jaw.

Thankfully, Jack popped in the door. "Good afternoon, honey. Hi, Dianne. How are you today?"

"Fine—I'm going to lie by the pool and wait for Bill to return from football practice."

"All right, dear. We're going to the supermarket," Ethel said.

Dianne put an innocent smile on her lips and walked away. *That woman is insane,* she thought. *I cannot believe she doesn't understand I have sex in her own home.*

It wasn't more than five minutes later that Bill came home from football. "There's my girl," he exclaimed as he rushed over to Dianne. "Looking swell, Dianne, just swell. Have you been getting some color?"

"I sure hope so—don't I look browner?" Dianne questioned as she peered at him under exactly two and a half coats of Maybelline mascara'ed eyes.

Bill smiled. "Guess what? Your parents just left for the grocery store. Which means...we have about an hour of alone time."

"Say no more." Dianne was already up out of her chair, running to the sliding glass door. A bobby pin fell out of her hair and hit the door's edge as Bill picked her up and whisked her inside the house. They started kissing immediately. Ever since that night at the drive-in, Bill and Dianne had been going at it like crazy. Going all the way had a whole new meaning. Rushing upstairs with Bill had always been a fantasy of Dianne's. Growing up as his neighbor, she had always dreamed that Bill would pay attention to her, so when she'd hit puberty, she had been pleasantly surprised. She'd gotten boobs, a boyfriend, and so much more than she had ever imagined at fourteen years old.

Bill gently laid her down on the bed and looked deeply into her intoxicating green eyes. "I love you, D. I really do." For the first time since her parents' divorce, a tear rose up in Dianne's eye. For the first time since her parents' divorce, a happy tear rose up in Dianne's eye.

At school the next day, Dianne decided to do what Ethel had asked of her and invite some of Bill's friends over for a goodbye party that Saturday night. It would be a "twist" party in the basement of the house, which Dianne thought was a little ridiculous, as Jack and Ethel would probably be home, but if they were cool with it, then that was groovy by her standards.

"So, when is this stupid thing?" Donna asked, throwing her cigarette butt on the floor and rubbing it in the ground with her loafers below her locker.

"Saturday night, seven o'clock," Dianne sighed wistfully.

"Girl, snap out of it. Bill is your guy; you should feel lucky. A guy like Bill, he will definitely get the Purple Heart or something."

Dianne gave Donna a serious look, saying, *Shut the hell up* with a mere flicker of her green eyes.

"All-star in high school, all-star in Vietnam," Donna said. Tears formed in Dianne's eyes; she put on her cat-eye sunglasses and quickly exited the conversation.

The next day, as Dianne helped Ethel make her famous snowball cookies for the party, she had a thought. "Mom?"

"Yes, Leslie," Ethel answered.

"Do you think Bill might give me a ring before he goes off to the war? Like, do you think he wants to marry me?"

"I don't know, sweetie," Ethel answered. "I know you two have been having fun and are going steady, but marriage? At your age?"

"Mommy, you know I'm not a little girl anymore. I've really developed these past few months being with Bill."

"Did you do the act yet?" Ethel inquired, with a wink and a nudge-nudge, forming the sugary dough into small balls.

"Mom!" Dianne shouted, feeling embarrassed yet quickly realizing she was trying to prove to her mother that she was an adult worthy of marriage. "Yes, in fact, we have," she replied, opening the wooden cabinet to get out the wax paper and powdered sugar to roll the dough in.

"Do you feel love when it happens?" Ethel questioned.

"Yes. I've known that I love Bill from the very second he put his hands on me. We are in love."

Ethel dropped the fortieth dough ball she had been prepping and gave Dianne a hug and a kiss, in one swift movement. Ethel looked nostalgic as she said, "That's exactly how I felt when I met your father. Did I ever tell you that story?"

"A million times, Mommy. Let's not ruin today by talking about Sy."

"You should call him your father, little Leslie," Ethel replied, quietly but steadily.

"Men aren't supposed to leave us girls," Dianne said, slowly, making eye contact with her mother. "That's why you married Jack—he will never leave us. I know that and you know that. Sy left us for good."

"He only lives twenty minutes away, Dianne. You can see him whenever you want."

The operative word being "want," Dianne said to herself.

"Open the oven, dear," Ethel requested. Wiping her hands on her pink-and-green floral apron, she said, "Now, we have just two hours to get you looking camera-ready for this party! Your hair appointment at Joanie and Ralph's is at five o'clock." Dianne and Ethel put their arms around each other and walked into the huge family bathroom off the kitchen to do makeup.

Two minutes later, Dianne came out flustered, with one eye set in blue liner. "Let me just set the timer, Mom!" *The last thing I need is to have burnt cookies at this party,* she thought.

As Dianne reached for the red timer in the shape of a hen, a bobby pin dropped out of her hair. She bent down to pick it up, and when she rose, she twisted the timer with a shaky hand. Her nerves were setting in.

Dianne looked up at the shelves above the big knobs on the old-fashioned stove and saw a picture of Jack and Ethel on their wedding day. She had seen it a million times before, but something was slightly different now. Each of their faces seemed so happy, so hopeful. If she squinted just far enough to the left, she could see herself and Bill posing together, fingers interlocked, Dianne wearing her mother's wedding gown and perfectly lace-encrusted bouffant. Dianne smiled and set the timer down. Tick, tick, tick. Time was running out.

*O*ne of the scariest things about growing up motherless is that you have no one who senses when something is right or wrong in your life. Moms have a special intuition for their children. And I didn't have any of that. I used to be jealous that my friends had moms to go shopping with, fight with as teenagers, and miss at sleepaway camp. When I became an adult, I just wished my mom were there to tell me if I was making a mistake or dating the wrong guy, or how to handle nausea from a UTI on a Saturday night. They should at least give you a damn powerful Magic 8 Ball the day your mother tragically dies. I hate how vulnerable all of it made me feel. I hated that I couldn't seem to protect myself from heartbreak. I hated that I couldn't ask her what to say, or how to say it, or who to be. I hated that I had no one to hug me unconditionally —ever.

But someday, redemption would appear. But in order for me to get there, I had to fall in love. I had to get to the point where staring at my phone was no longer relevant. Where having awkward pillow talk was useless. Where jealousy didn't rear its ugly head and make me feel as if I was one of millions of girls who could be right for the person I found so precious at the moment. I felt like I had spent so much of my life holding my breath, waiting for a response, hoping for more.

I always tried to imagine how my mother would handle heartbreak. My mom's best friend, Donna, helped me shed some light on it, but I still wondered. I remember noticing my mother tense up every time we drove past the naval base in San Diego and Camp Pendleton on drives home. Her tone changed every time. I never fully understood why until very recently.

After Bill's death, the military named the galley at Naval Base San Diego in his honor. Mercer Hall was dedicated to Bill on June 2, 1974. His brother, Van, told me that the Navy flew the entire Mercer clan out to California, including Van's newborn daughter, for the ceremony. It was a bright, sunny day, he relayed to me, and six years after Bill's death, the Mercers were relatively healed from the loss and humbled by the Navy's decision to honor Bill's legacy at a prominent military establishment. I should add that this particular naval base is one of the largest and most important in the United States.

Many nonmilitary personnel try to get a seat at Mercer Hall. I never thought I would be able to get onto the base without a major hassle from security. By then I had broken down so many barriers in my research that I was exhausted. Then a breakthrough happened: one serendipitous New Year's Eve, while I shared a late-night pizza dinner with friends in San Diego, three men approached us, asking if they could share our table, as the restaurant was very crowded. They were standing up, eating their pizza, and began to make casual conversation with us.

"What's going on, girls?" one asked. They were in their early twenties.

If I have learned anything by virtue of being a writer, it is to be polite to all and to speak to everyone. Even at three o'clock in the morning. After all, the six-degrees-of-separation theory has been validated repeatedly, both in my experience and in sociological research.

"How was your night, guys?" I asked, although I was too tired to be genuinely interested.

"It's been good, just glad to be off the base," one answered. His name was Kyle.

"Oh, are you guys in the navy?" my best friend asked. They all nodded.

"Oh my gosh," a tipsy version of my voice squealed. "Have you guys ever eaten at Mercer Hall?"

Again, they all nodded and, looking perplexed, asked me why and how I knew the name of their mess hall. "My mother used to date Bill Mercer, and that is who it's named after," I said, pride shining through my brown eyes. I almost felt like my mother, twirling her hair and singing "He's So Fine" into a mirror. I just wanted to tell these perfect strangers all about Bill. *This is wonderful*, I thought, grinning from ear to ear.

One said, "Did you guys know that this Mercer guy—"

"His name was Bill," I responded, cutting him off mid-sentence.

"Yeah, Bill . . . . Did you guys know he was a hero?"

"He received the Navy Cross," I informed them.

"Nice."

"In Vietnam," my best friend, Gigi, added, also gloating, as if we should be wearing I ♡ BILL T-shirts.

The guys slowly ate their pizza, undoubtedly surprised that they had just met young girls who knew all about the guy their mess hall had been named after.

"Can you guys get us on the base tomorrow?" I asked, before Gigi could give me her nonverbal look of *hell no, Jess.*

"Sure," one said, shrugging.

"Really!" I was virtually jumping up and down at this point, still seated on my stool. "She used to be a cheerleader," Gigi interjected.

"That's what I thought," one of the guys replied.

I laughed and rolled my eyes. "Really? We can go on the base?"

They all nodded. "Take down my number," the one named Kyle said.

I WOKE UP THE NEXT DAY WITH great anticipation. *I will finally get to see Mercer Hall,* I thought. I knew my mom would have loved to see it. I wondered if she actually had on one of our brief family trips to San Diego. Perhaps she had snuck out when everyone else was sleeping. But how could she have been granted permission to go on base? On second thought, my mother was amazingly resourceful and up to any challenge, so I have full faith that she could have gotten clearance somehow. As for me, it was pure luck that I had met three guys in a city I am rarely in, and that they had been hospitable enough to grant me permission to go on the base.

I called Kyle later that day and told him what time to expect us. The plan was still on. En route to the Coronado Naval Base,

I looked over at Gigi and said, "Thanks for coming with me."

"No problem. I want to see Mercer Hall, too," she replied.

I looked out at the ocean and saw my mom's face in the water for a second. She would have been thrilled to know I was on my way to see Bill's building. This was part of the payoff I had been waiting for after completing all of my research. I deserved to see Bill's legacy honored.

With a quick flash of our driver's licenses, we walked right onto the base, Kyle leading the way. The air was crisp, a cool breeze coming off the ocean. Old navy ships were on the harbor, and I could see Bill working on them, sweating and looking back out at the base where he would later be honored. Kyle probably thought I was nuts for having such enthusiasm, but I could not be concerned. I would have done anything for Bill.

"Here's your galley," Kyle said, pointing straight ahead to Mercer Hall. The old building looked its age, at least in part because of its dingy beige color. The building was framed in royal blue, a Navy color and also Bill's favorite. His name was emboldened five stories up. There it was: MERCER HALL.

I skipped ahead of my friend and Kyle, like a little girl entering a playground, and went straight to the entrance, until I was faced with a CLOSED sign. It was not a mealtime, and it was a holiday. "Shit," I said. "Let's go around back."

Kyle and my friend looked at each other and rolled their eyes as they followed me. They could sense my determination. There was no way I was letting anyone stop me from entering Mercer Hall. This visit was fifty years in the making and smelled like Saturday night at the Centinela Drive-In.

I walked right into the kitchen; no one was around. "You

can't just walk into a military facility," Kyle shouted after me.

"Oh, whatever," I retorted. He grabbed a cook's disposable white hat to enter, although for a second there I thought he was suggesting we go incognito to enter. I was down for that. Once my dramatic mind calmed down, I realized it was just for sanitary consideration.

Kyle ran smack into a cook, who looked very confused to see us. "She's a civilian," he said, pointing at me, and I waved with a goofy smile, "but she, uh, wants to see—"

I interrupted him: "Bill Mercer is my relative, and, well, I am visiting San Diego and want to look inside, please." The cook told us we could go ahead in; he did not seem to care either way. "Thanks!" And I continued my little-girl skip to the dining area.

The eating area very appropriately resembled a 1950s diner, with sparkly red stools and high tables. Each individual table had purple and yellow orchids on it. In the left-hand corner was a place for the "unknown soldier," set in honor of prisoners of war or soldiers missing in action. Bill was none of these; he was killed in action. There is no acronym for that—just the term "hero." I smiled, knowing Bill would be happy that this place setting was there. We goofed around, taking pictures at the tables and looking for the large oil painting of Bill. None of us could find the painting, so I approached an old Asian lady who was working there.

"Excuse me," I said to her. She looked at me, somewhat confused. "Bill Mercer was my relative, and I am looking for the oil painting of him."

"Ohh," she responded in her foreign accent. "You related to Bill Mercer? Wow," she said, smiling. *White is a pretty color for lies*, I thought, although I truly did feel related to Bill at that moment. "His picture used to be up outside, yes." She then went to the sliding glass doors, prying them open with a bat because she was too short to reach the lock.

"I could have reached that," Kyle said. We barely heard him. The three of us were too invested in finding Bill's painting.

The Asian lady told me that the painting had to be locked up somewhere because it was so old and valuable to the Navy. "They usually take it out and put it up on a movable plaque for special occasions in the VIP room," she added. My eyes sparkled with happiness as I thought of all of the generations of naval officers who had seen Bill's portrait every time they attended an event in that room. It pleased me so much that they were all aware of his valor. "Oh, Bill," I said softly to myself.

Moving into the VIP room, I smiled as I took a picture of the place where his painting was usually displayed. There was a mural of a bald eagle with a sky-blue background painted on the back wall. As I scanned the room, looking at all the empty chairs, I felt very much at home. I could feel Bill's presence as I contemplated all the men who had been in the firefight that had taken his life so many years ago. I silently recounted their names to myself, honoring them in a place I wished they could all have entered. Perhaps a few among those who had survived had. I felt privileged to be able to honor Bill. I wished only that my mom could have had the same experience.

Thanking Kyle and walking off the naval base, I felt a sense of accomplishment. I had never thought the world would lead me so effortlessly to Mercer Hall that weekend.

DIANNE

1965

A few weeks after the party, Dianne went to knock on Bill's door to surprise him and take him to pick up burgers and go to Dockweiler Beach to make out. It was their regular "thing" as a couple. Bill was leaving in a few weeks for boot camp, and Dianne was trying to savor every last moment. Dianne turned off her mother's Fairlane's ignition, even though she was too young to drive, and walked up to the door, bouncing her strawberry-blond curls for volume. She caught a glimpse of her own reflection in the stained-glass door and thought how good she still looked, even though she was so depressed.

Before she went to ring the bell, Dianne heard screaming. It reminded her of the moment she'd caught her parents fighting when she was five years old. These fights always seemed to have one thing in common: Dianne. The Mercer home had thin walls, and she heard Bill's mother.

"Bill, for God's sake, she is just trash. Trash—do you hear me? You are being a terrible role model for your little brother in these last days you are home! I don't even know my own son anymore," Maple sobbed.

"I love her, Mom. I know that bothers you," Bill retorted, with true emotion in his voice.

This was the billionth fight they had had about Dianne. The couple had managed to get into trouble from time to time, but Dianne always pulled through in the end. "Think about all the trouble you have gotten into, and how you stopped surfing. Your club needed you. You dropped the ball, Bill. It's time you grow up, and your first step is getting rid of that wretched girl."

"Okay, Mom. If that's what you want, I will break up with Dianne." Maple slammed a door. Dianne saw Bill spot her in the same window she had been gazing at her own reflection in just a minute before, feeling completely elated and in love. Now, mere seconds later, she felt completely betrayed and alone. "Dianne!" Bill shouted. But it was too late; she was gone, chugging down Yorktown Avenue in Ethel's Fairlane.

As the story goes, as soon as Bill broke it off with Dianne, Maple Mercer told her husband, "I would rather see Bill dead than married to Dianne." At ninety-two years old, Maple passed away regretting the utterance of that sentence.

Dianne went on to meet a boy named Glen Wayne Harber. He went by his middle name, just like she did. He was an attractive yet somewhat puny house painter. They met at a diner after a late night of dancing in Hollywood. She was with Donna. They had started to get into the Hollywood scene after Dianne's split from Bill. They had fun, and had lots of men and lots of sex, but it was never like what Dianne had had with Bill. Sure, sex always felt good, but it seldom included feelings of love.

Bill had been gone for three months, and they had been the

longest twelve weeks of Dianne's life. Even though she was seeing Wayne, she still thought of Bill, especially late at night. She felt like she was in her own war zone of combat, just waiting for the land mine of heartbreak to explode. When it did, it would probably be visible in the form of five pounds each on her ass and thighs. Dianne had heard around town that he was engaged to Trish, but she didn't care. She smirked when she passed Trish at the Sav-on ice cream counter. As Dianne licked her mint-chip cone, she made eyes at Trish, just knowing by the look on her face that she had never seen Bill naked.

Wayne was getting pretty serious about Dianne, and even though she was only fifteen, he wanted to marry her. Or maybe it was the other way around. Maybe Dianne baited Wayne to consider an engagement because she found out about Bill and Trish's. Or maybe Dianne just wanted a way out of Ethel's house, out of Westchester, and away from the memory of her and Bill. We'll never know for sure—Wayne passed away in 2002.

During the fifth month that Bill was in boot camp, he came home for the weekend. The first thing he did was phone Dianne. It had been nearly six months, and he could not bear another moment without her. He told her this. "Come over," she responded breezily, knowing he would be surprised.

Dianne looked at herself in her vanity, letting the light blue bulbs naturally highlight her cheekbones, wondering if she could really do this. Wayne was so into her, and he could potentially hurt Bill if he found out about this or any other sexual rendezvous.

Dianne told her mom to leave for a few hours, and Ethel obliged. "I'll just go over to Penney's and look at this season's dresses," she said, smiling.

"Sure," Dianne said, and closed the door. She stared hard at her reflection and got out a red negligee. Dousing rouge on her cheeks and matching her lips, she applied some mascara to her eyes but left it at that. She did not want Bill to think she was trying too hard for him. He did not deserve it. There was a slow knock at the door, three times. "It's me," Bill said, with a desperate tone in his voice.

"Oh, hi. I told you that you wouldn't stay away for long," she said with a sly smile, letting him in.

Bill and Dianne continued their late-night rendezvous while keeping up their other relationships on the surface. Maybe they had such complex personalities that they actually needed two people apiece to manage their emotional and physical desires. Or maybe they were just torn apart in a tragic-love-story type of way that only Shakespeare could write about. Even after Dianne married Wayne in 1965, she continued to see Bill as often as she could until he left for Vietnam in December 1966.

Dianne and Wayne's young marriage ended shortly afterward, in 1967. Getting divorced at seventeen years old estranged Dianne from world problems temporarily. Back at Ethel's house, Jack was watching the evening news. "Supposed to be on in two minutes, says Walter." Jack loved to call the newscasters by their first name.

"And now, real footage from Vietnam. Our troops are doing us proud," Walter said, with a lame smile and half a wink. Suddenly, Dianne was paralyzed standing up. She could not move a muscle, as she watched American soldiers moving slowly through treacherous rice paddy combat zones. She had to watch for Bill.

"I don't want you watching this, dear," Jack said. "I'll holler for you when it's over."

Dianne's hands were already over her eyes. She burst into tears. "Now, dear, I didn't mean to upset you," Jack said. "I know you're worried about that Mercer kid still. Oh, sweetheart, young love is hard to shake."

Suddenly, it was all over. Cronkite's voice returned. "That's just a bit we got from Khe Sanh, South Vietnam. This week, eight hundred and fifty-one US soldiers were killed," Cronkite said, flashing through several draft pictures in black and white. The men looked so young that the pictures reminded Dianne of picture day in the seventh grade at Orville Wright Middle School. "We managed to get five thousand Vietcong this week, so at least we are on the winning side." Kronkite finished with another grim grin, attempting to make it more serious but failing to. "Stay tuned for our local weather, folks. Here's a message from C and H sugar, the real sugarcane sugar."

Ethel walked in at that moment with grocery bags. "A little help, dear," she said, motioning to Jack. "I've almost gone and ruined my manicure." She laughed a little, glancing at her perfectly crimson-polished nails. "Leslie, how nice to see you here."

Dianne said nothing; she just ran to the mailbox. She had not received word from Bill in over six months. She had asked Ethel to save any letters for her. His silence was killing her. She was practically anticipating his death at this point. Her nails were taking the brunt of it. She was not herself. Fantasizing about Bill seemed pointless. Would she ever see his face again?

Six more months passed. It had been almost two years

since Bill had gone and almost one full year without correspondence. When Bill had first gotten to the war, they had exchanged love letters, but when he'd made plans to wed Trish in Hawaii on a military R&R trip, Dianne had not been able to bear keeping up with him any longer. Dianne had gone back to school but then taken another leave of absence, as she was too depressed to make decent marks any longer. A heartbroken seventeen-year-old divorcee was a recipe for disaster.

In an attempt to break her depression, Donna told her a funny story while they were waiting for their bowling lane to open one night. "Get this, D! You've got to hear this. There's a girl who went to our rival school who had great big hair. She was always getting in trouble for the height, but one day in homeroom, she passed out."

"From all the attention," Dianne sarcastically muttered through slurps of Coca-Cola, the bubbles still running over her tongue as she looked flatly at Donna, unimpressed with her story.

"No, listen," Donna went on. "So she passed out one day, and they went to let her hair down, thinking it would help her get more oxygen to her brain. Anyway, it turns out her artichoke 'do was so high that a cockroach had crawled in it one night and made babies in her hair!" Donna gasped as if she were hearing the story for the first time.

Shockingly, Dianne did laugh at this joke. It might have been her first laugh in ten months. "It's probably not true," Dianne replied, while still out of breath from laughing. "They probably just want to scare us from having good hair, and good men. That's why God made war, because he doesn't want us to get laid or be happy."

"Waah, waah, waaaaah," Donna said. "You're killing my game."

Dianne blew a big sigh of air through her French bangs and reapplied her lipstick. "I'm still your girl," she said with a slight smile, as she followed Donna into the arcade to socialize.

Dianne was stepping out of the Fairlane the next day, retightening a purple ribbon in her ponytail, when she saw Jack waiting for her at the door. Everything started to happen in slow motion and without sound, like in those Charlie Chaplin films.

"Dianne," he said, "I have some bad news." She nodded, barely moving her neck. "It's about Bill..." Jack's voice trailed off.

Dianne felt her heart sinking so low she could not feel it beating in her chest any longer. Instead, she felt her pulse pounding everywhere, all over her body. Jack continued to explain the way in which Bill had been killed. Dianne heard the terms "firefight" and "Navy Cross," but she could not digest the story.

Cars were passing on the street, lined with purple jacarandas in full bloom. A butterfly fluttered by. Dianne wanted to be alone and went straight to her room, staying there until the next morning.

The next day, when she went into the kitchen, the *Westchester Daily News* told Dianne where Bill's funeral would be. Even though she was not invited, she had to be there. At the cemetery, Dianne nestled herself atop a grassy knoll, slightly hidden behind an evergreen tree. She gazed briefly at Trish, weeping beyond control. Dianne knew in her heart that she was Bill's real widow.

I was finally going to meet Donna for the first time, although finding her was not easy.

One of my nephews had been up until three in the morning watching *Cars* because he had a head cold and could not sleep. I had slept over the night before, as I was babysitting and my sister was busy with work. "Move over, Auntie Jess—my side," he had demanded at one in the morning. *Oh lord, this will be a long night*, I'd groaned to myself. But upon waking the next day, I'd felt the right amount of distracted.

I had been in touch with Donna for nearly a year. That meant it had taken her nearly twelve months to find the time to see me. Unfortunately, for this key witness, I had to be very patient. In truth, finding Donna was my "come to Jesus" moment. I had struggled to do research about my mother's life for several years. I had pussyfooted around, always coming down on myself for being curious, and had put it off, thinking, *Mom didn't want me to know all of this, or else she would have told me.* But there was more to it than that. There were underlying social pressures and psychological factors that prevented her from disclosing many things to my sister and me. Like any good mother, she wanted to shield us from certain ugly truths of her upbringing. Now that I was a grown woman, however, I knew the time had come for me to find some answers from the most trusted source—my mom's best friend since kindergarten.

Stepping into the shower, I tried to brainstorm what I would ask Donna. *What will she look like?* As I scrubbed the shampoo through my hair, the part of me that was apprehensive wished I could wash away my curiosity just as easily as I rinsed the soap out of my hair. It occurred to me that my life experience has been analogous to the fine hair I inherited from my mother: beautiful but often tangled. I remembered when my mom would brush my hair each morning before school. It was so hard to manage. "Were there rats sucking on your hair last night?" she would ask. I would get so grossed out, thinking about rats running along my headboard, coming up to build a nest in my hair. *I'll probably ask my own daughter the same question,* I realized with a smile.

"Auntie Jess! Let's put on makeup!" My nephews came rushing into the bathroom as I began to take out my makeup. "Not today, babies, I am in a big hurry." I had overslept that morning because I had a nightmare I could not get out of. I dreamed I was on ecstasy and kept taking it like an antibiotic—every four to six hours. I kept trying to stop and get out of the high, but every time I tried, my thinking became more clouded. I felt so out of control.

I threw on my blue dress and put on my mother's pearls, first into the left ear, then the right. I liked to think they brought me luck, but I wore them almost every day, and I didn't consider myself particularly lucky at all. I mean, they even forgot my order at the Coffee Bean sometimes. Taking one final look at myself in the mirror, I grabbed my overnight bag and headed downstairs. My sister was feeding her kids breakfast and, the nanny had just arrived. The ratio of adults to kids had reached an acceptable standard, and I so I set off on my way.

"Bye everyone! See you tomorrow. Wish me luck."

"Bye, Ah Jah," my middle nephew screamed. "Wuv you."

My first stop was to visit my grandmother in Orange County. We would either eat lunch together or play cards. May I? was the name of the game. It was what Sicilians called Crazy Rummy. Every time I saw my grandma, she asked me if I had learned how to play Texas Hold 'Em yet. I always told her my life was like Texas Hold 'Em—men were bluffing me all over town—but she did not get the sarcasm.

Walking into the house I grew up in, the house that I no longer considered to be my home, I saw Grandma Ann through the dining room windows, sitting in the backyard.

"Hiya, Jessica—you look beau-tee-ful!"

Grandma Ann was the epitome of the perfect grand-mother. She was hands down the most wonderful, giving, and thoughtful human being who ever existed, and I loved her with all my heart. She knew about my project but could not keep up with it, because, among other health complications, she could not hear a thing, even with her hearing aids on level four (full blast). She lived with my father in the same house I grew up in, which had no remnants of my mother's life there. I used to think it would be upsetting to return to that house, but it never was. It may have been strange, but the impact of our extreme loss was somehow muted there.

As my grandma and I sat outside in the backyard, playing May I?, I routinely told her what day it was. She looked concerned, and then sad. And then went back to telling me how old she was, and still kicked my ass in the card game.

Suddenly, my father emerged. We had been fighting the week before. It was always a struggle with him. He came down with a pile of bills in his hands that he then went through in front of me. From the look on his face, I could tell it was not in a "let's go through these papers while I visit with my daughter" way. Instead, it was "look how strained I am right now."

He looked at me and said, "There are only two hundred thousand books published each year."

"Wow, really? I feel like that's a lot," I replied.

"What's your backup plan, Jess?" he asked. I ignored him. It was those kinds of comments that kept driving a wedge between us. I left my dad's house feeling a little depressed, but more inspired than ever to meet Donna.

I stopped for lunch in Laguna Beach, at the Surf 'n Sand Hotel, a Barraco family landmark. My mom had been vacationing there since she was a child, and my parents went there on their honeymoon. My brother-in-law proposed to my sister there, and whoever decided to commit to me would have to carry on the tradition. That hotel was a special place.

Overlooking the deep blue Pacific Ocean, I was greeted by my best friend, Gigi. "Here you go." She handed me a gift-shop bag.

"What is this?" I asked.

"You know I shop when I'm bored," she said flatly, with a smile.

"A magnet! How cute."

"Yeah, it can go with your 'we've already got the something blue' flyer on your refrigerator from the Surf 'n Sand's wedding promotion," she replied, rolling her eyes and raising one eyebrow.

"Perfect!"

Gigi and I had the best sarcastic banter. Whenever we were around each other, we reverted to our usual personalities, however much had changed. I was always the positive, energetic, hopeful, yet painfully depressed one who wanted to get married, and she was the girl who, even when she couldn't seem to catch a break in life, could whip everyone around with her wit and be there for them. Like, really care and be there. She had been my best friend for ten years.

We took the elevator down to the ocean level to have lunch at Splashes. Ordering a skirt steak and a shrimp butter-leaf salad, we talked about how life sucked and what I should ask Donna. I was really hoping my best friend would know what to ask my mom's best friend. Gazing out at the blue ocean, I saw my mom and me laughing and playing on the shore, so long ago. The cookies 'n cream milkshake. The waves. So many waves.

"Here's your entrée, girls," the waitress exclaimed, interrupting my deep thoughts. I blinked and let myself out of the memory. Gigi knew better than to interrupt me whenever I zoned out. "Never get in the way of a writer and her thoughts," she said. My eyes blinked back to reality. "Looks good," I said, not really caring about the food.

Toward the end of the meal, I walked to the bathroom. The intricate white windowpanes, which revealed the crashing waves, secured so many memories. I saw my family in the right window table, eating a Mother's Day meal. My mom was wearing a floral scarf to cover the tracheal hole in her throat, and my family was eating politely, pretending that our matriarch was not in severe pain. She did not want us to feel bad for her. She was not a woman who tolerated self-inflicted pity.

The sun hit my face as I came out of the bathroom, and I realized just how important this day was. *Donna will know everything*, I thought.

Driving to Donna's home in San Diego, I reflected on how I —or, rather, Sam, my ex-boyfriend—had originally located her. For a long time I could not write or research because it reminded me of him too much. Sam believed in my research. He had somehow found Donna on the Internet, and I had called her number four times that night. She had not answered. One night a few weeks later, I was at dinner with my uncle. He pressed me to call and leave a message. What was there to lose? If it wasn't the right Donna, she wouldn't call, but if it was, she would definitely return my message.

When I called her that night, I got her machine again. "Hi, this is Dianne Barraco's daughter, Jessica. We have never met, but I am interested in learning more about my mom and just wanted to ask you a couple of questions. Please call me back if this is you; if not, I apologize for wasting your time."

About a week later, she returned my call, and my whole life turned upside down, in more ways than one. I had just gotten into what seemed like the thousandth argument with Sam. I went home from his apartment and got the phone call from Donna.

What impeccable timing. I stopped stewing over Sam and

our issues to notice: when I needed hope, it called me back. I was so happy that it was the right Donna that I suddenly forgot how terrible our fight had been, and all I wanted to do was kiss him and thank him for making me believe in this project. A few minutes later, Sam walked in and I said to him, "You found Donna! It's her. Thank you, thank you, thank you so much!" I was truly elated.

Sam ignored my happy mood. "I saw someone's car parked outside, and a guy your age got out of it and flipped me off. Any idea who that would be?" he asked. This must have been the fifth time he had accused me of cheating on him, which I never had and never would.

"You know all of my guy friends. Did it look like anyone you know? I was up here talking to Donna, and before that fighting with you. How could I have had time to screw someone in between?" He did not like that answer, but I was at my wits' end with his insecurities.

"I'm happy you found Donna, but I'm really upset right now," he said, as he sank into the couch.

"I made you dinner. Are you hungry?" I asked, with a hint of "I should have broken up with you three months ago" in my voice.

"No, thanks. Maybe later. I need to ask you something."

For the love of God, I thought. I had just rehashed each and every one of his insecurities from the past six months in the last three hours. *What could he possibly be upset about now?* He always needed reassurance; he always needed help in handling his emotions, but what about me? What was in it for me besides Donna?

"That dream you had, where you saw your fiancé in New York, and you didn't think it was me ...," he began.

I interjected, "Did you break into my diary?" My diary was computerized at that point. I had grown sick of handwriting my issues about our volatile relationship. There was too much to write. Something about "Dear Diary" just didn't cheer me up the way it had when I was fourteen.

"Well, the file was open on your computer."

"Oh my god, I can't believe it," I said, and then repeated it maybe four or ten times more.

"That's not the point," he said.

"Yes, actually, it is the point. That is my personal space that you do not invade. How dare you!"

"How dare *me*?" he shouted. "How dare *you* for keeping that from me!"

"It was a dream, Sam—big fucking deal. I think it's quite apparent we wouldn't be happily married at this point. I don't lie to my own diary, since you read it. I don't know who the man was in the dream. I wish I did, believe me," I said, getting more and more strident with every breath.

Sam then got up without acknowledging me. He passed the dinner I had made him, unmoved by the tears in my eyes.

I could not tolerate this exhausting relationship any longer. He opened the door, and I slammed it shut—I was not going to have my neighbors hear yet another one of our alter-cations.

"Owwwwwww!" he screamed, more loudly than anything I'd ever heard before. My mom had had seizures in our house, and yet I had never heard screams like that. "You broke my fingers!" he shouted at me.

Grabbing the pizza I'd made him and throwing it on the floor, he paced in my tiny kitchen until he tripped himself and fell flat on his back. "Oh my god, stop screaming! We'll just get some ice."

"You cheated on me! You probably don't even remember who you slept with, and you dreamed about marrying him!" he screamed, with wails of pain in between.

I was sobbing, on my knees, with a bag of frozen peas in my hands. Not the best Kodak moment. "No, I didn't. I would never cheat on you! Why don't you believe me? I know we're over, but please believe me," I told him with hopeful eyes, eyes that I'd given him a million times before, eyes that he would never believe. At that moment, I finally accepted my own painful expression and knew that enough was enough.

"Call the paramedics," he demanded. "I'm afraid of you; you meant to injure me."

"You must be joking," I said.

I grew up in a house of trauma. I know what an emergency looks like—the tension and fear that quickly build, and the feeling that there is nothing you can do anymore. This was not one of those times.

"Call them *now!*" he roared.

I was scared. I went into my room and, with shaking hands, dialed 911 on my landline. The operator answered. "Hi, this is not an emergency, but my boyfriend—"

"I'm not your fucking boyfriend anymore!" Sam screamed in the background.

"He slammed his fingers in the door, and he's in a lot of pain." I hung up.

The paramedics arrived quickly and took a look at his fingers. Sam had finally stopped wailing and crying. "Can you bend them, son?" one of them asked. He bent one finger. Then he bent all of them, including the ones I had allegedly slammed in the door on purpose. "You might want to go to your doctor tomorrow and get an X-ray or two, but your fingers are just fine," the paramedic said.

"I want to go to the hospital. She'll take me," he said, as he nodded over to me. I didn't know whether to laugh or to cry.

"Have a nice night, you two," the paramedics said as they walked out of my apartment.

I couldn't believe how quickly the tides had changed between us. "Let's go. Now!" Sam demanded.

I put on my clothes with absolutely no intention of taking him to the hospital. In the elevator ride downstairs, he said, "You know last week on *Dexter* the serial killer tortured his own son by slamming his fingers in the door? Sound familiar?"

The doors to my lobby opened up, and I said, calmly and quietly, "I will drop you off at the hospital, or you can drive yourself, but there is no way in hell I'm staying with you." I pressed the button to go back to my floor.

I could hear Sam screaming profanities through the closed double doors. That day marked the first day in my life I really chose myself, and it started with pressing the number three in my apartment elevator.

As I arrived in San Diego, I was in a wonderful frame of mind, having that ugly experience behind me. Relationships had always been frightening to me. I had never felt safe or truly respected in them. But Sam had led me to Donna, and to me finding Donna was worth the drama he had put me through.

Donna was waiting outside her trailer home, flagging me down as I pulled into a parking spot. Funny thing about trailer parks: they are the only places in Southern California where finding a parking spot is not an issue. Donna gave me a bear hug as I walked briskly up to her. I held in the moment and thanked all of the benevolent powers in this universe that I was finally with her. I looked at her, at her big hair and her large green eyes, reminiscent of my mother's. In her face I saw a strong woman who had lived a tough life. "Come on in. It's so great to see you," Donna exclaimed.

I had never been to a trailer park before. I was under the impression that trailers moved. Wasn't that the whole point of them? I guessed not, because the dark wood base was planted firmly in the park with the other Mountain View estates. I felt like I was entering Eminem's past in 8 Mile, but seeing the inside decor and knowing that my mom had been there all those years ago made me feel immediately comfortable. I wondered what the walls would say if they could talk. The interior reflected displacement and loss. I saw a birdcage with no bird, and a giant cat-furniture-type maze but no cat. I contemplated the fact that animals might or might not have lived in the house at all.

She seemed cheerful as she apologized for having not seen me for so long, because of a knee injury that she finally had under control. She told me how she had to ask her neighbor to take her to and from the hospital because she didn't have a spouse or companion. My heart twinged a little bit, hoping that this was not my future. Being in and out of relationships was routine for my mom and Donna. Just like eating breakfast, lunch, and dinner. Nothing sounded less appetizing to me.

"I read a letter you wrote to my mom about fifteen years ago," I said, after taking a few sips of water.

Donna's face lit up. "Oh, yes, we used to write letters to each other." I smiled, remembering how my mom would check the mail avidly when she was expecting a letter from Donna and, upon receiving one, would run upstairs to her room, sit on the right side of the '80s-colored peach-and-moss-green bedspread, and instruct me to leave her alone. She was a great mother but, like all people, needed some alone time. "Can't I just lie here?" I would ask, picking apart the tiny strings of fabric.

"No, please give me a few minutes." I would hear my mom laughing, making her signature snort, which sounded like it came from the back of her throat but really was from deep in her soul.

"What did the letter say?" Donna asked me, bringing me back to reality in the trailer.

"Oh, it was funny—you were telling my mom about a boyfriend you met at a wake or something."

Donna's face looked flabbergasted, and then softly fond. "Gee, I forgot about that. Randy! I met him at a wake, and he called me that night and asked me out, and it turns out it was his mother's wake. Would you believe that?" she said. "I need to smoke. I'll be back."

"No problem," I said, scrounging for my notebook so I could take down the scenery. Donna and I had been sitting on a comfortable beige couch directly next to her kitchen . Still no sign of the elusive cat that Donna had told me she took for walks every day, on a leash, no less. In the back, there was a bedroom converted into a nail salon where Donna did her neighbors' nails once in a while, but not so much anymore, she told me. The bathroom had a mirror covering the shower doors. I had never seen anything like it before.

After marrying for a short while, Donna had eventually raised her only son by herself. "Was it difficult?" I asked her when she returned with a picture of him.

She shook her head no. "It's hard not having someone now, though, to grow old with. If I did, I'd retire with him, maybe take one of those cruises." I was speechless for the first time during our visit.

A few seconds later, we finally got to the subject of Dianne Barraco—or Dianne Taylor or Dianne Bradshaw, as she would introduce herself to neighborhood boys who asked her on dates. The Taylor name was after the great Liz Taylor. Clearly ahead of her time, my mom would have loved Carrie Bradshaw on *Sex and the City*.

My mother was always a few steps ahead, even as a teenager. Dianne and Donna would make up fake phone numbers for boys they were just "flirting" with but had no intention of dating. When my mother got her driver's permit at fifteen and a half, Ethel allowed her to drive the car but did not tell Jack, who would have been the voice of reason. Ethel let them take her car, a heavily chromed Fairlane, and they would drive to Westwood or Beverly Hills to shop, or travel to Hollywood to go out clubbing. "We would leave the house, waving to Ethel, with a look that said, *See ya at 2:00 a.m.*—wink, wink." Donna wink, winked at me as she talked. "She just let us go."

The two girls were inseparable from the time they met in kindergarten at Cowan Avenue Elementary School. "Why do you think at five years old you were drawn to each other?" I challenged Donna.

"It's funny how you don't realize how much you know yourself at five years old—it's true what they say."

"What's that?" I asked.

"Your personality really does stop developing then." Donna laughed and gave me her ear-to-ear grin, which within just twenty minutes had become as familiar to me as that of a lifelong friend. "In school, there are cliques, and we had our own," Donna commented. "We were like exclusive, hip loners." She went on to say that she and my mother simply had other interests, that it was hard to be truly interesting in the early 1960s, when everyone was trying to fit his or her own family's version of a square. The world was so chaotic at the time that individuals had created strict order in their homes and families to compensate for the inconsistencies of outside forces that were beyond their control. Amid drug use, rock 'n roll, and the Vietnam War, people from that time had no choice but to hunker down, accept reality, while also trying to escape what was looming.

As I scribbled down notes, Donna seemed a bit nervous. "I hope I'm saying the right things, since you're taking such careful notes."

"Donna," I told her, "I wouldn't be writing this book if it weren't for you. You made me believe that all of this was possible."

Donna smiled, looking both relieved and shocked. "Now that I think of it, your mother and Ethel had more of a typical Jewish mother-child relationship," she said. "I didn't know until all these shows on TV started popping up. I thought it was weird then, because my mother was so conservative."

"So they were more like friends?" I asked.

"Yes," she smiled. "Best friends."

Ethel and Dianne had a girlfriend relationship, sarcastic yet kind. They would "bitch about" neighbors, boys, and the latest hair and makeup trends, bouffants and heavy blue eye shadow. Donna helped me see the difference as she described her own mother. Mrs. Brown was a strict Lutheran woman who was quite conservative, especially after Donna's father died when she was thirteen. Oftentimes Donna would get grounded for seeing my mother, because they only got in trouble when they were together. When that happened, Ethel would find a way for them to reconnect.

"Ethel was an enabler. Your mom and I probably wouldn't have been such a powerful team if it weren't for her help." Donna recalled that whenever she was grounded, Ethel would have my mother's stepbrother call for Donna and ask her over to his house, because Mrs. Brown would not be able to distinguish Lucky's voice as that of Dianne's stepbrother.

"My mom used to limit how large my hair would get," said Donna. "The ratted, big hair was in style then. But Ethel would help us get our hair bigger!" She got up to describe how large my mother's bathroom was: "humongous—like, twice this living room."

"We would douse ourselves in perfume, rat our hair up with thick combs, and work the smoky cat eye." Donna's eyes dazzled as she explained this to me. "Your mother was vain."

So am I, I thought but didn't say aloud. This was something I had been hearing for a long time. The Leibowitz girls (Ethel and Florence) were vain. They lived to get their hair done and would not exit the house without a perfectly pressed outfit and a fresh face of makeup on.

"We were obsessed with clothes. Oh, did we love clothes. In fact one time, we shoplifted," Donna continued.

Now, this *is what I drove to San Diego for*, I thought. *The good stuff, finally.*

"One day, we took the bus into Westwood Village and found ourselves in an expensive boutique," Donna remembered. "I'm talkin' expensive clothes—fine fabrics from France and such." A slight twinkle in her eye developed as she continued. "We were about thirteen or fourteen years old," she said.

"Now, why did you shoplift?" I asked. "Did your parents not give you an allowance?"

"No, they did," Donna said. "We did it for the thrill."

Donna and my mother were in a clothing store on Broxton Avenue, and, as the memory unfolded into greater detail, I could almost see the snooty saleswoman looking at these "ratty teenagers" who were, of course, oblivious to her withering stare. They either didn't notice they were out of place or didn't care to acknowledge it. My mom wanted to steal a lavender silk dress that they could go out clubbing in. She and Donna wore the same size. She had managed to hand the dress over to Donna, who was carrying an oversize brown bag, when the saleswoman confronted them with a sharp glance.

"What do you girls think you are doing?" the saleswoman scowled, as she dialed the police. I recalled how my mother's uncle was the police chief of their district at the time, and I wondered if this had crossed my mom's mind at all. Dianne and Donna started laughing hysterically and waited for the police to come and get them. When the officers arrived, they hauled the girls down to the station. Dianne and Donna saw it as a thrill even to be in a police car, and then in the station.

"We were giddy from the adrenaline rush, I guess." Donna

chuckled and flashed her signature grin again. "Well, then we arrived at the station and our parents met us there."

Ethel was not particularly shaken up, Donna recalled, but her mother was. Since this was around the same time her father had passed away and other family troubles were brewing, Donna still could not remember why they might have committed such a crime. "Why does anybody commit a crime like that?" she asked. "No one really needs to do it."

I nodded, thinking how I should have used that as the thesis for one of my criminology papers in college.

"Your mom and I were so giddy, down at the station, that she picked up one of the officer's guns and held it at me, faking like she was holding me up." She squealed a little. "Oh, how funny that was. We were laughin' so hard, we were cryin'. Excuse me—I need to go around back and take another puff of my cigarette."

I looked around the room and felt grounded by a calm realization that my mom had had a wonderful friend in Donna.

"Now, where was I?" asked Donna upon her return.

"Tell me about when you girls would go out in Hollywood," I pressed.

"Oh, I don't know if I can tell you about that."

I thought, *You just told me you shoplifted in Westwood for the thrill of it and staged a police holdup at the station. What could be worse?*

As Donna combed through my mother's relationship with Bill Mercer, her warm smile faded. For a moment I wondered if she might resent me for reminding her of lost youth. "Bill was a big dude, as I recall," said Donna. "I see him having a solid, large build and light hair. He was the longest relationship your mother had until your dad. We got wild around fourteen and fifteen."

I told her my assumption that Bill's death caused my mom to act out, become delinquent, and eventually drop out of school. "We used to prank-call people in the neighborhood, sending liquor orders to real conservative people's houses." Donna laughed.

"Why?" I asked.

"We were thrill-seekers," she said.

"That brings us to 1965," I said.

"We lost touch," Donna responded. "That's when she met Wayne." Glen "Wayne" Harber, who was born on December 28, 1945, had been my mother's first husband. Donna described him as a "goofy, small, unattractive" guy. He and my mother lived at four different addresses. Much to my astonishment, their last residence turned out to be my last place of work, at a public relations agency at 340 Main Street in Venice.

"I don't really remember her being married," said Donna. "All I know is they skipped town for a short while. I don't know if it was to scare your grandmother into letting them get married underage, or if there was a baby or a miscarriage, but they were definitely gone." Having a half sibling was something I had long ago considered and ruled out. Given the amount of research I had done, birth records would have shown up. Of course, there could have been a miscarriage or a private adoption, in which case they wouldn't have. Donna spoke about the "shady abortion clinics" that inhabited LA at the time. I envisioned a hippie woman in a dirty lab coat, with hair draped to her buttocks, ushering young girls into back rooms where a creepy doctor coldly completed the procedure.

"Once your mother came back, we both lived in the Mar Vista and Venice areas, near the canals," Donna said. "I remember her giving me plates that she got as wedding presents, but she didn't want them. They were white, just plain dishes; I probably still have them here right now," she chuckled.

It seemed to me my mother's marriage happened strictly out of rebellion. "Quite a rebound from Bill, huh?" I responded.

Donna smiled and said, "See how well you know your mom? She would have read you like a book, too."

After another hour of reminiscing about the good old days with Donna, I felt the chords of "Cherry Bomb" in the air. Even though both Donna and my mom shared rough times, together and apart, I was so happy that my mom overcame those challenges to live her own life and to be the wonderful, resourceful mother she was for my sister and me. She had so many fantastic experiences to draw from. I could only wish that she had not been so embarrassed of them. Pride was a strong thing. Both of them enjoyed a reckless lifestyle. Donna found sheer pleasure in it and continued living it for a while, but for my mom, it represented something else: failure. If only I could discover the catalyst for it all. If only I could find Frank Parker.

"So, you both used to ballroom-dance?" I questioned Donna.

"Oh, you know it! I used to go dancing down in San Diego to earn some extra cash. We would win, like, fifty bucks at the clubs," she said, enthusiasm rising in her voice. "We would dance the cha-cha, the hustle, disco-type routines—your mom and I loved Motown," all of which she said in the same full breath.

"I know you did. As a little girl I went and saw Smokey Robinson and Gladys Knight perform in Las Vegas," I said.

"Gee, that must have been neat. I watch *Dancing with the Stars* and think about your mom."

"I know! My sister and I always talk about how much she would have loved it. It's on tonight," I said.

Donna nodded, looking at me with a distant, vacant stare.

"Donna, you know today is the anniversary of her death. She's been gone for eleven years." Suddenly, the emotions became overpowering, the tension palpable. I could almost see my mother's spirit drawing Donna and me together as she burst into tears.

"I loved your mother; I loved her. I really did."

I got up to hug her, as tears also formed in my eyes. "I know you did, I know you did. We all did. And she would be so happy to see us together right now," I said, still not entirely convinced that was true. Because people who knew my mother didn't hear her discuss her life, they made me feel like she might have been disappointed in my curiosity. But, as with the times before, I brushed it off and took a deep breath.

Donna left again to smoke a cigarette as I wiped my mascara-drenched eyelashes. I took out my hand mirror, which I secretly hated but could not seem to get rid of. Jake had bought it for me for me on my nineteenth birthday—his first gift. It was a silver compact mirror, engraved with my name on the front and my birth date on the back. *How much did I actually ever love him?* I wondered, but the moment passed as Donna returned.

Reminding myself of the main reason why I was on my quest, I asked her, "Do you remember Frank Parker?"

"Yes, I do." She smiled. "Your mother loved him so much. It was like"—she touched her heart—"*the* guy in her life. The big one." I nodded. "How did you find out about him?" Donna asked.

"My father told me about their affair after she died; I also remember her telling me about him when I was really young."

"Frank was a good man. I can see him right now: dark and extremely good-looking. Probably the best-looking man your mother ever dated," she said.

I told Donna how frustrated I was that I had not been able to determine the correct timeline. I could not seem to figure out when they had met. After a little best-friend reflecting, she said they had to have met and been together between 1967 and 1970. The story goes that Frank moved to San Francisco for work in 1970, and my mom could not leave Ethel, as she was sick with Parkinson's and recovering from a stroke.

I pictured their having a tearful goodbye but my mom being strong. I could see Frank driving off into the distance in a black convertible, gearing to drive up the coast of California, wishing my mom could be right there next to him. She had the freedom to go, but she felt strongly committed to stay with her mother, who had stood by her when she was "troubled." Guilt had been a monumental driving force in her life, as it was in my own. The butterfly burst through her chrysalis alone and taught herself how to pump her own wings. But her family still controlled which flower petal she flew away from—the petal that had been her only known birthplace and home.

Through Donna's experiences, I drew some conclusions. "Your mom and I were doin' the same thing, but in two separate cities."

"The true test of best friends," I said with a twinkle in my eye.

Donna nodded. "We used to sit in the living room, doing choreography and practicing our routines until they were flawless. You know, we had a number of boyfriends. We'd go from man to man; it was for the thrill of romance. But once the magic was gone, things would be done in about six months," she said.

"How did my mom deal with heartbreak?" I asked. This could have been my most burning question. All of the times my heart had broken, I'd wondered what my mom had done to comfort herself.

I closed my eyes for a moment and saw my mom with medium-length brown hair with blond streaks, drumming her nails on the table in her bedroom, drinking a martini. She would finally get fed up with herself and blow some air up through her French bangs, put on a green dress—her signature color, to match her dazzling eyes—and go out dancing. Yet no man would ever top Frank on the dance floor, or in life.

"So, I understand why my mom could not have ended up with Bill—he died in the war—but why didn't she end up with Frank? He clearly returned to LA eventually," I asked.

"I really don't know, Jessica. I wish I did," Donna answered with a sigh.

As adults, Dianne called Donna from the hospital when she was sick and did not want her daughters visiting her. She would call not to complain but to reminisce about old times. As my mother's body slowly shut down, afflicted as she was from one devastating autoimmune disease after another, battling cancer and its effects for longer than she got to see me alive, Donna continued to be uplifted by my mother's friendship.

My mom understood that Donna could not visit her often, tied down as she was by her own personal problems. In times of weakness, my mom was stronger than Donna and was emotionally supportive of her, just as she had been in the '50s and '60s. Donna believed the foundation they had laid as children, as wild as it may have been, created the trajectory of a lifetime of friendship. "Even when we didn't see each other, we were still always each other's best friends," Donna said. "Life is funny that way."

*D*ianne woke up to her dog, Shadow, barking more loudly than she ever had before. "What do you need, girl? I'm trying to sleep."

"I'll get her," said Ray, Dianne's new boyfriend. She had met him on a girls' trip to Palm Springs the previous month. He was from Maryland and had already flown out to California to visit her. *How exciting is that?* Dianne thought. She was so in love. She was in love with love. Ray seemed uncomplicated, down to earth, and happy-go-lucky. None of the men she had met before had possessed such comforting qualities. Dianne always feared Ray would leave her, even though his stay was open-ended. She did not want to risk hoping too much.

"I'll go—just go back to sleep," she said, as she kissed his cheek. Sweeping her platinum blond–dyed hair into a messy bun and getting the red dog collar out of the kitchen drawer, she stumbled through her Mar Vista apartment. "Shadow, come out to the courtyard. Come on," she said, while motioning toward the door. Shadow was already directly behind her. Instead of being one step ahead, like her owner, Shadow was always one step behind. Dianne wondered if all adorable black poodles behaved this way. She would never know, as she'd had Shadow spayed as soon as she could.

I wish I could get spayed, Dianne thought to herself. Sex was always getting her into trouble. As she twisted the gold knob on her cream-colored door, she wondered if sex would get her into trouble with Ray as well. Dianne was naturally so sensual and free-spirited that she sometimes pondered how sex would change her relationship, but she never considered what a relationship would be like without it, because that would be a relationship not worth having. *If you are going to be with someone, why hold back?* she thought. It was not in her nature to hold back.

"Shadow, are you done? It's freezing out here." Never a dog lover, Dianne had adopted Shadow in a time of need. She needed to feel love from a living thing that needed her, could not live without her, and wouldn't leave her. Someone had told her that a dog could fill that void better than a human being could.

Shadow was still sniffing around the courtyard. Dianne felt a chill from the wind. Nights like these, she could feel Bill in the wind. Dianne was astonished at how much she still missed him and that nearly ten years after his death she still could not shake the love they had shared. She had tried to replicate it with every other relationship, but nothing could ever measure up to her first love and the sheer bliss of experiencing those feelings for the first time. Dianne could definitely have won the medal for "Forced Relationships and Failed Triumphs in Love," if one of those had existed somewhere, over all contenders. After Bill died, Dianne's life had taken a turn for the worse.

Wayne was the first man Dianne had met after Bill. He was

a skinny, brown-haired, nineteen-year-old painter. Dianne was still only sixteen. The fact that Ethel did not approve of their relationship led Dianne to flee the state and added still more scandal to her already disreputable image as a young high school dropout whose life was defined by Hollywood partying, illicit cocktails, and drugs—all of which was driven by her angst over her lost love in Vietnam. She had never gotten to marry Bill, so why not marry the next man who treated her with some affection and respect? Legend has it that Dianne and Wayne fled to Idaho for a couple of weeks and either married there or threatened not to come home until Ethel agreed to legally vouch for the marriage.

As the story goes, Ethel was going out of her mind back in Westchester, crying to Jack every night, asking how she could have gone so wrong as a mother. Her sixteen-year-old had no education and had fled the state. "I just have to give her what she wants so she will come back," Ethel sobbed to Jack in a moment of clarity. She had grown tired of constantly crying and agonizing about it all.

Dianne's little stunt worked. Just about fifteen days after Dianne and Wayne had crossed the Idaho state line, Ethel phoned and said, "Okay, Leslie. I will sign for you to marry Wayne." Dianne's face lit up. She would get a marriage after all that year. Wayne was one hell of a rebound, to say the least.

"SHADOW, I AM DONE WITH this courtyard. Do you hear me?" Ruminating about things alone in the dark was one of Dianne's guilty pleasures. She considered how well she had done moving beyond the mistakes of her youth. Wayne had turned out to be a royal mistake. Dianne had found love with Bill and lust with Wayne and had been too young to tell the difference. And now she felt anger.

"Shadow! Now!" Shadow scampered in right behind Dianne, riding her pink-slippered heels. She knew one thing for sure: Ray would never know about Wayne.

The next day, Dianne and Ray took Shadow for a walk in the neighborhood. "Shadow, sit." The poodle jumped up. "Shadow, give me your paw." She growled. Ray tried to do the same, and he was just as ineffective.

They both laughed, until they noticed a stocky man with furrowed brows across the courtyard staring at them. He was holding the metal chain of his pit bull very tightly as he told it to sit, stay, and heel.

"How the fuck does he get him to do that?" Dianne wondered out loud. And then they both saw it: he used brutal force. The stocky man nearly pulled the larynx out of the dog's jugular to make it sit or stay. Dianne thought animal control should pick him up. Without thinking, she approached the man.

"Excuse me, sir? What the hell do you think you're doing to your dog? Do you just like to see how loud you can make it whimper?" Hands on hips, Dianne gave the man her usual *don't even fuck with me* squint with her green eyes.

"Who do you think you are speaking to?" the stocky man demanded.

"I am your neighbor, Dianne Harber, living in 2C, and this is dog abuse. You are cruel. Now tell me, who the hell are you?"

The man walked away smugly. Dianne was a firecracker to say the least, and always said what she wanted.

Ray and Shadow were playing fetch with a tennis ball. Dianne could not have known then that most of her life would be this way: fighting her own battles.

A woman emerged from across the courtyard, wanting to pet Shadow. "That dog is just precious," she said in a jolly voice to Dianne.

"Hello there," Dianne said, embarrassed at how flustered she looked.

"Gloria Segal," she said, putting her hand out to shake. Dianne shook it and felt an instant connection with her.

"Nice to meet you," Dianne said. This never happened to her. She felt a powerful bond with a woman who had actually calmed her nerves enough to make her forget she was in the middle of bitching out her neighbor.

"We should go get a drink sometime," Gloria said to Dianne, clearly feeling the same connection Dianne had felt seconds before. The same man had followed Gloria outside of the house. "I have got to run; it's dinnertime. Bye now," Gloria said, with a cheerful grin.

"Dinner," Dianne thought aloud. "Dinner! Oh, shit, I have to get ready for work."

Dinner reminded Dianne of work because dinner was her work.

Ray followed her in disbelief, and he fed Shadow while Dianne went into the bedroom to get dressed. "Oh, shoot. Where's my brown skirt? Ray, is it in the laundry basket?" Dianne yelled, distressed, from the bedroom.

"I think this is it. Why does it look so big?"

"Hey, watch it there, boy," Dianne said, smiling at him in her lace bra and underwear, reaching for the oversize brown skirt with tulle ruffles underneath.

"Do you work at an amusement park?" Ray joked.

"Something like that," Dianne replied, giving him a quick kiss on the nose. Dianne rushed back into the bedroom and reappeared five minutes later, tying a Windsor knot in a tangerine-colored silk tie.

"Whoa, you can tie that fast," Ray said, as Dianne non-chalantly tightened her tie without looking in the mirror.

Touching the magenta velveteen couch with her hands, Dianne scooted Shadow off the furniture and picked up her server's jacket.

"Let's go," she said, grabbing the keys off the flowery metal key rack. Ray followed along her heels, mimicking Shadow. It was 1974, and the beat went on.

When Dianne ushered Ray in through the back of the Westside Broiler, her beloved place of work, busboys, bartenders, and waitresses greeted him. Marcy, one of Dianne's closest friends at the restaurant, was the first to scream, "D! Are you kidding me? What a doll he is!" Marcy squealed right in front of him, like only a mother would. Dianne felt herself blush a bit.

"Nice to meet you," Ray said, with a smile. "I just got in from Maryland a few days ago, and I'm here to eat...dinner?" He gave Dianne a confused look.

"Oh, Ray." Dianne rolled her eyes. "Come with me out front; I want you to meet Bryan."

"Look, here he is now. Ray, this is Bryan, my manager. Bryan, this is my new friend, Ray."

"How do you do," Bryan said, with a quick yet indifferent smile. "Pleasure to have you at the Broiler."

Ray opened his mouth to say something, but Bryan interjected: "Dianne, you have a call party tonight. Rock is coming by."

Dianne did a little celebratory jig. "Who's Rock?" Ray asked.

"Rock Hudson," Dianne and Bryan both said in unison, looking at Ray like he was an alien.

"Gee, the actor, you mean?"

"You're in Los Angeles, baby—of course the actor. He has a crush on me," Dianne said proudly. "I better go steal one of Marcy's pressed aprons," she added, as she rushed off the dining room floor.

"You can pick Dianne up around midnight," Bryan said. "It's going to be a long night."

"Stevie Wonder came in one night and played on that piano," Dianne told Ray on his way out, as she briskly walking in with her freshly pressed apron on and red lipstick outlining her Cupid's bow and making her green eyes jut out more.

"I'm going to need a dirty martini later, Miguel," she said, cupping her mouth so her voice could project to the bar. This was her territory, and she was proud to be the ruler of the roost. Miguel smiled.

Just then, a panic came over the crowd socializing around the mahogany-paneled bar. Dianne heard small sighs from the ladies and watched all of the men in the room straighten their ties to witness the arrival of a Hollywood icon.

"Let me get the door for you, Mr. Hudson," said Norma, the greeter. Norma was known to be "very hot," according to the regular customers. She always worked the door because, well, it worked. She was a tall, beautiful woman of Spanish descent. She had a model's legs—long enough to span from Barcelona to the tip of Ibiza, where the party always started.

"Dianne! Hello, lovely lady." Rock approached Dianne as she stood by the piano with Ray by her side.

"Good evening, Rock. It's a pleasure."

"Seating at table eleven, Dianne," Norma said quickly, in a hushed tone, before she escorted Rock and his male friend to the best table on the floor. Nina was wearing sheer black nylons with an exposed seam up the back of her calves. Dianne wished she could wear that type of hosiery to work. She bit her lip thinking of how happy she had once been in Norma's hosiery, dancing with her partner all night long.

She smiled, reapplied her red lipstick, blotted it, and walked onto the black-and-white-tiled floor where her night would begin. After Rock put in his order, and the party after him, and the party after that, and the last spinach salad was spun tableside, and the last gong for freshly brewed coffee was rung, Dianne was exhausted. She was ready to take her new boyfriend home.

"Nice job tonight with that nasty party in the corner," Bryan said to Dianne as she took off her apron and hung it in the large closet.

"Thanks, Bryan," she said. "It was nothing. Say, what do you think of Ray?" Dianne was always looking for people's approval of new boyfriends because she felt she could not completely trust her own judgment. Was it her judgment, or was she just learning?

"He seems nice."

Dianne stood against the back wall with her hands crossed on her chest, furrowing her brow.

"Did I piss you off?" Bryan asked.

She shook her head no. "I piss me off."

Bryan looked confused as Dianne walked into the bar area just to see Ray walking in, soaking wet. "Is it raining outside?" Dianne asked.

"Looks like it." Ray smiled at her.

What was I so worried about? Dianne wondered. *This man is an excellent specimen.* "Let's go home." Dianne walked with Ray, hand in hand, out of the Broiler.

"I love driving in the rain," Dianne said, once they were in the car.

"Quite a strange comment for a California girl," Ray replied.

"My mom and I used to listen to the rain together on nights when there was thunder and lightning," Dianne said. "I always imagined listening to the rain with my daughter someday, under the covers," she continued, in a dreamlike state.

They smiled at each other in the way that two people can only do when they are both feeling the same euphoria. Dianne felt a rush of emotion that she hadn't had since Bill had left. She felt extreme love; she would no longer need anyone else's approval about Ray. She was going to marry this man. Her sense of certainty arose in that beautiful moment of just driving home from work with him, in the rain, and singing along to a song they both knew. *I've finally found my match,* she thought, as a tear fell from her kaleidoscope eyes.

JESSICA
Fall 2010

I was having dinner with a friend when I received a call from an unknown number. It was Regina.

"It's so lovely to talk with you," she exclaimed, in a very innocent and soft-spoken voice. We carried on a forty-five-minute conversation that was helpful, but she was not in the Jewish community, so was less likely to know my mother or Ethel well.

But, Regina had a great memory of Westchester proper, including all of the store names. Among all of the older people I had spoken with, the ones who could accurately recall street and department-store names were few and far between. So when Regina started talking about "the southwest corner of Manchester and Sepulveda," I knew she would be a great resource. I eagerly wrote down all of the names of ice cream parlors, bowling alleys, and dress shops.

"Joan and Ralph's is where, like, everyone went to get their hair done for prom," she recalled.

Based on her explanations, I have a vision of the town of

Westchester. I see my mom strolling through the Penney's with Donna and going to grab a burger at Tiny Naylor's with Bill. I see Lucky pushing the second ice cream scoop off the top of my mom's cone at Thrifty and laughing hysterically. I see my mom and Bill holding hands at the Loyola movie theater. I see glimmers of childhood happiness and simplicity.

"Thank you so much for this, Regina."

I got back to my evening. There were so many characters in my story that sometimes I just needed to pretend that one of them might not be so relevant. But I was wrong. Months later, I was up late e-mailing Regina and waiting for Frank to appear before our very eyes.

My mom and I collectively spent too much of our lives waiting and searching for one man: Frank Parker. Part of me despised him because he would not come out of hiding, and the other half of me wanted to find him more than I was willing to admit. I had become addicted to him, just as my mom had so many years ago. I was getting help from a friend who was a lawyer, this time to access LexisNexis.

I had recently discovered that the company Frank had worked for was prosecuted by the United States in a highly publicized, national trial that lasted over ten years. The company's chief executive officer was accused of several counts of loan fraud, conspiracy, falsifying corporate records to company accountants, and more. This white-collar criminal had begun to serve ninety months in prison just two years prior to the start of my search for Frank Parker.

I learned the name of the company by first tracking down my mother's friend Gloria. It was a rainy day in the fall. It had occurred to me that finding Gloria might help my chances of finding Frank. By then I was so good at searching for people on the Internet that I found Gloria's number in less than two minutes. I dialed the Palm Springs area code and waited.

"Hello," said the same deep, jolly voice that I had heard in so many family videos.

"Gloria? It's Jessica Barraco. How are you?"

"Oh my word. Jessica? You sound so grown up!"

I winced a bit at her reaction. This was everyone's reaction, and it was beginning to grate on me. It reminded me of something I did not like to think about: how so many of these people disappeared after my mother's death, even though I was still just a little girl then.

Gloria and I spent the better part of an hour catching up. How was her son; how was my sister; how was her husband, Ed? When I felt we had established a comfortable rapport, I told her what I was looking for.

She took a long pause and then said, "You know, Ed and I used to take some television and radio parts to swap meets in the area, and one of the times we went, your mom gave us a business card of a friend. His name was Frank."

Encouraged, I said, "Go on."

"It said he worked for a company called Columbus Recreation, Inc. Frank worked as a salesman in their warehouse or somethin' like that," she said, with a bit of a hick's drawl. "I got the impression, you know, that your mother and Frank were involved somehow, but I did not know about the affair. No, I did not." Her voice got more and more nasal.

I could tell she was choking up thinking about her friendship with my mom and wishing she were still alive to confide in. I bit my nail and then stopped, knowing my mom would have swatted my finger out of my mouth if she had been there with me. "So, Gloria, do you think I can find this company still?"

Of course, the prospects of finding Frank remained daunting. All I knew was that his company hadn't gone through the simple bankruptcy that was typical of gadget companies in the 1990s that were by then already in strong competition with web-based companies. The real story was more convoluted—and intriguing. I had told myself I would stop looking for him a week prior to my speaking with Gloria. But I couldn't quit my intoxicating, by-then-obsessive search. I considered the possibilities: Was he in a witness protection program? Of course, it was much more likely he had simply left town when his company was busted. Even if I were to establish contact with the company president in prison or someone else who had known Frank in passing, would that make him any more accessible to me in modern day?

It was one o'clock in the morning. Regina had informed me via e-mail that she had a friend who was a U.S. marshal who could find out which prison the company president was in. I told her that I was chicken-shit at the prospect of talking to an inmate. I just wasn't comfortable taking my investigation inside prison walls. My detective muse, Nancy Drew, would not have been caught dead in her platform heels walking into the maximum-security prison in Florence, Colorado, right? I lived my investigation vicariously through Nancy Drew, always questioning, *What would Nancy do?* Neither Nancy nor I had received any formal training, but we both possessed killer intuition.

Regina tracked down the company president's address in

prison. What would I do with it? I could write to him but didn't know if it would be worth the hassle or the risk. He was probably not going to know Frank's middle initial or have his phone number. The former president could potentially reach out to his ex-wife, who might have the human resources records, but I felt sure that she and other former business associates wanted nothing to do with him or the case.

As it started to rain, I heard it beating down on my brain, saying, *You will never find Frank. He will never come out of hiding.* Frank was such a common name. It was also the former president of Columbus Recreations' name. What if Frank had been the president and my mom had given him another last name to protect his identity? That would be classic—and also very annoying.

Later that week, after an early-morning spin class, I received an e-mail from Regina. She gave me information that would lead me to the president's ex-wife, Elizabeth. I had read about this woman in a news article and had seen how the company's bankruptcy had ripped their marriage and family apart. Elizabeth had tried to get some money, using a powerful attorney, in the first part of the trial, which had taken place about ten years prior. Regina's research revealed that Elizabeth had become a wedding coordinator at a church in Long Beach.

Right after spinning, when I was high on life and endorphins, I gave Elizabeth a call. Not surprising, but worth noting, was that Regina had even given me her correct extension. She answered right away.

"Can I speak with Elizabeth, please?"

"This is she."

Oh, shit, I said to myself, and then quickly recovered. I

played what I call the "my mother is dead" card and stated that I didn't care about her ex-husband, the fact that he was in prison, or his very public trial for being a corporate scoundrel.

Elizabeth spoke to me for about five minutes. I realized early on that she was not going to tell me if Frank's name was familiar, even if it did resonate with her. Regina had instructed me to leave my phone number in case anything crossed her mind later, so I did.

In despair, I called Regina and complained to her for the next half hour. In her schoolteacher-polite voice, she told me that I could go to the county registrar and search old voting records to see if I could find Frank that way. "Do you want to come with me?" I asked, half kidding and half hoping she would say yes. She agreed!

I spent the rest of the afternoon talking to Kim, the psychic, on the phone. She had shared her impressions about Frank with me before, and I needed to see her again as soon as possible. She had told me that she sensed he was either dead or living in a quiet, dusty town where people go to be forgotten. She thought a place like Modesto, California, would be a good place to start.

I didn't want to give up on Frank. He was simply too important to my mom, and to me. I had to continue my search for him. I always felt that when I found Frank, I would get the answers I had been looking for and would then be able to process all of the information I had found, and all of these insights into my mother's life, and my own would coalesce. I would be able to spread my own butterfly wings, burst through the chrysalis of Southern California, and fly away.

I t took Regina and me weeks to find Elizabeth, but the lead was dead in less than five minutes. So goes life. Within a few days of my fruitless conversation with Elizabeth, I went to see Kim and she channeled my mother when she told me of one of my mother's jewelry boxes I used to play with. "There's a jewelry box with a treasure inside it," Kim said. But I was worn out from searching.

Four days later, I went to Orange County to see my grandmother. I brought her a poinsettia, her favorite Christmas plant.

About half an hour passed. My dad entered the kitchen again, the same kitchen where my mother made her famous tuna-noodle casserole and stuffed bell peppers, but I could not envision her cooking there anymore. That memory had been replaced by vague memories of my grandma cooking for me in high school, at the kitchen table where she was spending her platinum years playing Skip-Bo and sipping hot chocolate through a straw.

To my astonishment, my dad was carrying my mom's

jewelry box that Kim told me about days before ... and handing it to me. My heart stopped in my chest. It was like seeing a ghost; I hadn't seen that jewelry box in over ten years.

"Dad, this is my only happy childhood memory. I used to play with this for hours in Mom's room with her." He looked at me, checked the box for anything valuable and said, "Fine, you can have it." At first glance it appeared to contain nothing of value, but I knew what each pendant and semiprecious stone had meant to my mother. I could surmise where she might have worn these pieces, and with what outfits. And I could fantasize about the outfits she wore that predated my memory of her walk-in closet.

As I took possession of my mother's treasure chest, I remembered that, when I was a little girl, my mom motioned me to sit down on the floor and opened the large mahogany, gold-handled jewelry box she loved. There were only a few times I was allowed to play with the items in it, and every time I did, it was like stepping out of my life and into a dream. Those '80s clip-on earrings really did the trick for me. How I loved trying them on! The sheer size of the earrings doubled the size of my tiny earlobes, and I would brainstorm about what clothes I could steal to match each pair. I had a keen fashion sense at a very young age.

Then I reflected on my father. Would he really let me keep it? The last time I'd asked him for something of my mother's, he had handed me the box of memorabilia from her funeral. Rummaging through condolence card after condolence card and eventually stumbling upon her death certificate, I'd shaken my head, frustrated, wondering whether I would ever find something of hers that had genuine meaning for me. The memories I had were fading quickly.

Of course, I could still evoke all of the times my mother had sat me down on her peach stool in the bathroom and curled my hair for dance class and recitals. I loved to inhale the Sebastian hairspray as she tried to do my hair as well as a professional might, using her royal-blue, fine-toothed comb to tease up the volume. I thought it was too much volume for a young girl, but it certainly held up during those shows and tap routines.

One time, my mom was curling my bangs and burned my forehead by accident. Oh, how I cried. "Don't worry, Jess. I'll get the tomato, like Celia taught us." My mom loved picking up natural remedies from other cultures. I have to say, if you ever get a mild burn, immediately apply the inside of a tomato. Nothing else takes away the pain faster. Quickly returning, out of breath and ruining her own curled bangs, my mom squeezed tomato pulp onto my small forehead. Ugh, I didn't want it to get in my eyes. For, as much as my mom primped, I was very much her little primper-in-training.

After we covered up my burn with some makeup, I was good to go. Lipstick was my favorite part. And then the spritzing would come. My mother would ever so gently pick up her Rive Gauche perfume and put it on her inner wrists and neck.

Back then, I would try to sneak into her walk-in closet and get to the mahogany jewelry chest. Going through it, I knew, would remind me of all the fun I'd had, and of all the envy I felt for my mother's beauty, which was one of a kind, a very Ava Gardner–esque, inspiring beauty that radiated warmth and made everyone smile. I had gazed at her multiple reflections looking back at me from the mirrored walls and closets behind us. It looked like an enchanted fun house to my mind.

I could not wait to rummage through the box, and finally

had my chance when I got home that night. First, I took a deep breath of the velveteen lining and smelled Rive Gauche. I peered into every nook and cranny, feeling up the sides and the pouches, hoping to hit the jackpot with something super sentimental or beautiful. If I had looked in the mirror, I would have half expected to see the six-year-old version of me. That's how I felt. The box evoked sweet, tranquil memories.

I found several things that I'd definitely wear. Most notable: a pair of pear-shaped jade earrings. I had been looking for a distinctive everyday item, and the 1970s earrings, back in style, fit the bill beautifully. I also found an old, dusty ring of Ethel's that was copper or gold. As I remembered all of the times my mother had shared some of her past with me, I couldn't help but think, *My mother's heart is my life.*

When my mother would get sick and have to enter long hospital stays, many of which, unfortunately, coincided with Mother's Day or her birthday (they were in consecutive months), she would spray a pillowcase with her scent before leaving—the best "miss you" medication imaginable. In college, I sprayed Jake's cologne on my pillow when our relationship went long-distance. It was the best thing to go to bed with— well, second best to Rive Gauche.

Next, I found a bottle of Rive Gauche. I inhaled it deeply and saw her sparkling emerald eyes as she applied her makeup. *Dare I spritz the air with it?* I chose to do so. Soon, the space was filled with a very powerful, lost memory: My mother was closing the door, saying she loved me at least five times and telling me to count to eighty-four. I had trouble falling asleep and would also stay up worrying about her, but she would help me by telling me to count numbers, as I was then too "grown-up" to count sheep. In the morning, she would come in and wake me up, eating her beloved toast with jelly and Swiss. She would walk in with curlers, saying, "Get up—time to start the day!" I was never a morning person and did not fully understand how much she truly had to appreciate every day she felt relatively okay. Looking back, I saw she really did know how to live life fully, and to stay present in the moment. She taught us all how to enjoy life.

I remembered I got very nervous before my dance recitals at the Barclay Theater. My mom missed her dancing days and never got to perform in recitals as a child. I realized that she was living vicariously through me during my performances, of which I had magical memories. I was so anxious, trying to distract myself by evaluating the other girls' body types and rummaging through my mom's makeup bag. "Now, now, relax," she would tell me. "You're going to look gah-geous," she'd say, with a fake New York accent. I felt awkward with blush and lipstick on, but when she put that mascara brush to my eyes, I felt beautiful and exotic. I desperately wanted to know what I would look like as a teenager, and as a woman. I hoped it would be very much as I appeared with mascara on.

My mom had to leave the backstage area an hour before the show because the classes rehearsed right until each class's performance call time. I would bite my nails nervously as I peered out into the dark theater from the stage, only to jump back behind the heavy red velvet curtain. Suddenly I'd be transported into my own world. The only thing comparable to performing onstage is sex. It's possible to remember doing it, without being consciously aware of the sequence of motions. In both cases, only the beginning and the ending are memorable.

Of course, as a ten-year-old, I had no idea what to compare performing to; all I remember is wondering if I had done a good job or not. All of the girls would rush backstage in their jazz, ballet, and tap shoes, the air smelling like Aqua Net hairspray and perfume. Wondering if I'd missed any steps, and tasting the Clinique red lipstick on my small mouth, I felt a rush of adrenaline. I would be half worried and already half embarrassed that I had made a mistake in the routine, as my teachers sometimes frowned at us backstage. But then I would see my beautiful bouquet of red roses and the sweet note in my mother's handwriting. "You were amazing, Jess! We are so proud of you. Love, Mommy and Daddy."

The year my mother passed away, my father escorted me to the theater on the night of the spring recital. We were about thirty minutes late. Sadly, I did my own makeup and hair; my mom had taught me well. I can vividly remember running backstage after the performance, adrenaline pumping, and seeing other girls getting flowers. Where were mine? Sweat poured from my sprayed-down, stiff hair. *There must be a mistake*, I thought. I knew my mom had a lot to do with the bouquet coordination after each performance, but I did not realize it was all her. I was not greeted with a note from my mother, my one and only fan and inspiration to dance and perform. I was not greeted with anything but perspiring emptiness.

I stopped dancing in 2001 because of that loss, and it came to be something I hugely regret. At the time, I just was not strong enough to endure one more thing in my life that reminded me of my mother's absence. Shakespeare once said a rose is a rose by any other name. And for me, heartbreak was heartbreak, by every conceivable name—even tap class.

A bout a week after they first met, Dianne took Gloria up on her offer to have a drink.

"Ed's not coming home until seven tonight. Come on over," Gloria said in her jolly voice.

Dianne hung up the phone, flung her hair to the side, and checked on Shadow. She was sound asleep, and so was Ray. She walked up the back stairs in her yellow platform pumps and knocked on the door.

Gloria answered immediately, holding two glasses of neat scotches. "I hope you like Glenlivet."

"It's my favorite," Dianne exclaimed.

"Good. You can have it at your restaurant, because tonight we're drinking the cheap stuff!" Gloria laughed at her corny joke, and Dianne didn't know whether to join in or walk out the door.

Dianne walked into Gloria's home, taking in the musty furniture, the brown and beige couches that looked old yet homey. Dianne took the ice-cold drink Gloria offered and examined the glass closely, which had small, perforated holes in it. She swished the yellow liquid and looked at her watch. Four o'clock—Ray was definitely still sleeping.

"So, how did you meet this visitor you have? Tell me all about it," Gloria said, as she sat down on the couch next to Dianne.

"It's a very funny story, actually. We met a few months ago when I was in Palm Springs," Dianne replied, waiting for Gloria's judgmental reaction. Most people would say, "Met a guy on vacation? Are you kidding?" Surprisingly, Gloria did nothing of the sort.

"That's great! Wow. I love that," Gloria said.

"Yes, I get to Palm Springs often," Dianne replied. "And I love seeing concerts—in fact, I saw Elvis last month." Dianne straightened out her dress. She was always walking the fine line between being a lady and being a fun party girl.

"Gee! Elvis Presley," Gloria said, in disbelief. She shook her head. "I have never seen a really good concert like that before. I want to see Billy Joel."

She gazed at the raised, spider-pronged diamond ring on her right hand. Her ring, she explained to her friend, had gotten stuck somewhere, and Ray had been the only man who offered to help her.

Gloria smiled. "Well, isn't this a nice story? And what did you two do after that?"

"We went out dancing." Dianne was getting more comfortable with Gloria. "See, I used to be a ballroom dance partner—I had a partner and everything," she said, her eyes widening. "We danced the cha-cha, salsa, everything. We did it all," she finished, taking a sip of her drink, and realizing how the conversation had switched so quickly and so personally.

"It must be serious if he came to visit you from Maryland," Gloria said.

Dianne did not think this was a big deal, especially in those days. Plane tickets cost a fraction of what they do now. The choice was simple to her: Did she want to whine about travel cost or experience love?

Just then, the wooden door opened. It was Ed, looking grumpy and flustered. "Gloria, I'm hungry. Is dinner ready?"

"Um, I was just leaving," Dianne said, as she gulped down the last of her cheap scotch.

"Dianne, you don't have to go so soon," Gloria said. Ed had gone into the bedroom to change.

"It's fine, Gloria, really. Thank you for having me."

Just as quickly as Ed had entered, Dianne exited. She had the night off anyhow and wanted to see how quick Ray was on his feet. People always seemed more fun on vacation, and she wanted to make sure Ray could match her pace in Los Angeles.

On the short walk back through the courtyard filled with ivy lacing its way up the cast-iron gates, Dianne thought about the last serious relationship she'd had before Ray. *Frank Parker.* No one could ever have been a better dancer than he. At twenty-five years old, Dianne thought she knew it all. She had thought she knew it all at eighteen, when she had met Frank, too. She thought she knew how a man should touch her and hold her, but she had no idea how that could be. Growing up, she'd always believed she might be a professional dancer, but until Frank came into her life, she had received no recognition for her talent. With him, she did. They would go out dancing at clubs along the marina and in Hermosa Beach and win money and trophies for doing the cha-cha or salsa.

The night they had first met, she had been wearing a strapless red dress and had caught Frank's eye. He might have told her she looked like one of the *West Side Story* actresses; maybe he didn't. Maybe that was just the look she was going for, and she saw the spark in his eye that showed his attraction to sexy women who could dance. She didn't remember what he was wearing—plus, she'd been rather intoxicated—but she did remember his moves. *Five, six, seven, eight, double-time.* Dianne saw them in her mind's eye, dancing in her living room, with the intention of practicing some new choreography for later that night, and making love in the kitchen instead. It was one of those rare times when two people are so in sync with each other that they don't need much rehearsing. The chemistry would balance out any potential missed steps. Maybe Dianne smoothed over his black silk shirt and he took the lint off the back of her dress. Maybe Frank came up behind her and kissed her neck, as she said, "Hey, don't kiss the perfume off." Dianne's one splurge every six months. Nothing else compared to her signature scent.

Lost in the reverie, Dianne didn't realize she was back in her apartment. She had automatically opened the door and petted Shadow. Ray was in the shower.

Snap out of it, Dianne told herself. Frank was gone, and he was not coming back for her.

"I thought we could go dancing and get some dinner," she yelled through the steamy bathroom.

"Sounds good, honey!" Ray was happy.

Was Dianne in love again? Was she ready to give up on the Frank fantasy? Would she even want to have children with him if he did come back for her? Ray seemed like a stable man, and she imagined he would be an outstanding father. She could easily see them having a family together, and she liked that. Ray was different from the others: she did not have to worry about him. Ray was the one man Dianne had met who she believed actually wanted to be in a serious, committed relationship with her. He was so available.

Dianne was complicated. Dianne had that something special: a groove to her strut, a spark in her eye. He was impressed with things like her sophisticated awareness of all that Los Angeles had to offer, and her unnerving intuition about people. People were drawn to her like a moth was to light. Her intensity burned many, though it was never her intention.

It was the '70s, so Ray put on his best platform shoes and vinyl pants, ready to head out for a night on the town. Dianne chose to wear her strapless red dress, the same one she had worn when she'd met Frank. She shook her head in the mirror, trying to come up with a good justification for the outfit choice. Raising her left brow, she finally came up with *I'm going to create new memories in this dress, memories that have nothing to do with Frank.*

Soon, they were at the club. Tom Jones's baritone voice filled the air as Dianne and Ray entered a nearby lounge. "Come on, babe, let's dance!" Ray pulled her onto the dance floor before she had a chance to decide whether she wanted to stay there. She always liked to scope the scene out, but tonight, she was also trying to scope herself out. Ray was a good dancer for never having had any training, but Frank had been better.

That's all right, Dianne thought, as he twirled her around and nearly fell over his bell-bottoms. She laughed, and then remembered how happy she was. She could never have felt this way with Frank, or else it would have lasted, she thought. She knew this was true, too. So by the time Captain and Tennille's "Love Will Keep Us Together" came on, Dianne held Ray close, inhaling his Lagerfeld cologne, and took a deep breath that said, *Goodbye, Frank. Forever.*

*I*n their first few years of marriage, Dianne continued to work at the Westside Broiler. She and Ray led opposite lifestyles: Ray was on his feet all day, pounding the pavement to pay the bills, and Dianne was a waitress whose shift started at 6:00 p.m. She would oftentimes catch a drink with her work friends afterward and not make it home until four in the morning. Ray understood that they had opposite schedules, but what he could not understand was catching Dianne coming home with a man who looked a lot like the man in her ballroom-dancing photographs. They were just friends, she assured him. But even to Ray's innocent eye, he looked a lot like Frank, the one with whom she'd shared so many trophy wins and years. Ray was not a jealous man, but the intense times he knew she and Frank had shared made him aware that it would not be safe for them to spend time together alone. And why would they, he reasoned. Was it not true that Frank had abandoned her when her mom was ill? Ray was the only man who had promised not to leave her. Why would Dianne ever go back to Frank? Old habits die hard.

Before leaving for work one night, Dianne checked her

long, wavy, platinum-blond hair in the mirror. *Gosh, I should have redyed it this weekend*, she thought. Visible roots were not in style in 1980. Glancing down at her nude-colored nail polish, she wondered, *What would my nails look like if I didn't have to work with my hands all the time?* Quickly opening the turquoise notch on her lipstick case, she lacquered her lips with a crimson color. Then she dotted the same color on her cheeks and gently rubbed.

Giving herself a once-over in the mirror, she rushed to start dinner for her three-year-old daughter, my sister: mac 'n cheese and fish sticks. Dianne did not have time for anything special these days.

In walked Ray, wearing sweatpants and a button-down, blue-and-green pin-striped dress shirt. When Dianne called him, he came—even if he desperately wanted to shower and change first. "I feel like I never get to see you—you come home so late," Ray said.

"You know we have to keep this lifestyle going, honey." With sad eyes, Ray agreed, giving her a long, warm kiss goodbye.

As Dianne turned on the ignition of her blue Mustang, she felt a twinge of guilt, knowing what she was about to do was worth it, despite the incessant scolding from her friends and family. She whipped out the perfume she hid in the car and spritzed it on one wrist and then the other, warming up her skin to make sure the scent sank in as deeply as possible. Throwing the perfume in her purse, she sped down Anise Avenue, the very same street she used to drive her mother's Fairlane down ten years before, what seemed like a lifetime ago.

Swiveling into her parking space outside the Broiler,

Dianne walked up the steps and entered the restaurant. Gazing off into space, Dianne got chills thinking about that one night, so many years ago, when the song, "My Cherie Amour" was the only sound they could hear besides the beating of their own hearts.

The fantasy was halted short by Lily, a pocket-size German lady who ran the hostess table and was in charge of reservations. "Running late, my dear?" Lily inquired. "You look like you're in another world right now."

Dianne laughed, wondering how long she could realistically keep her secret up. "Hello, Lily. I hardly sleep during the day anymore—which means I don't sleep at all! I'm just tired." She grinned. "Lily, where's Bryan tonight? I've got to tell him that if Muhammad comes in, I don't want to be his server." Dianne was referring to the boxer Muhammad Ali, who frequented the restaurant at least once a week.

Lily looked surprised. "Dianne, come on! Have you ever met a man who passed on an opportunity to be with you?" Dianne laughed.

*N*early thirty years later, I entered what had become Lawry's Prime Rib in Beverly Hills, and what used to be the Westside Broiler, and approached the bar with Sam by my side. I had called ahead to the current manager, mentioned that my mother was a Lawry's alumna, and said I wanted to have the waitress who had been there the longest serve me. Lawry's believes in having an old-school restaurant experience, which is quite a rarity in Los Angeles.

We had a few minutes to kill, so I ordered a glass of pinot noir from a small Mexican bartender named Miguel. "You look so familiar, *señorita*," he told me.

"I do?"

"Yes, *sí*. Like someone I knew a long time ago. Very pretty." He smiled.

"How long have you worked here, Miguel?" I questioned. Sam was in the bathroom.

"Forty years," he said.

I smiled, wanting to high-five him. "Then perhaps you knew my mother, Dianne Barraco?"

Miguel stared at me for a good few seconds. He had stopped pouring the wine into the large-bodied glass. "No kidding! I have pictures of Dianne and me. Your mama! Wow. We used to go party—you know, out dancing, everything." He kept giggling to himself. "She was crazy, you know. Lots of fun!"

I nod. "I know. I can't believe you remember her! How is your family?" I suddenly felt compelled to have a conversation with Miguel.

"They good, you know. Four kids, lots of grandbabies."

"Miss Barraco," a hostess interrupted us. "Your table is ready."

Miguel told me he would come visit our table later. Sam and I were ushered to the back kitchen, exactly where my mom undoubtedly picked up her tables' meals. As I carefully scanned the back bar, I spotted the freezer, the large refrigerator, and I could almost hear my mom's laugh in the air.

I was then introduced to the staff: "This is Jessica. Her mother used to work here many years ago, so please take good care of her." Everyone beamed and waved at me. Nowhere else could you possibly get better service; it was just impossible. Sam looked flabbergasted by the warm greeting, but I had expected it.

We were greeted next by a waitress who had been working at Lawry's for twenty-eight years, just two years shy of serving steaks and prime rib with my mother. Her name was Gina. I told her that I was looking for people who knew my mother, and while she did not, over the course of the meal, she came up with the name of the former costume lady, Mrs. Feathers, who might remember my mom.

"Feathers does not work here anymore, but she would be happy to talk to you. She has pictures of all the waitresses. She kept very conscientious tabs," Gina assured me.

"Great!" I was smiling, happy we had come to Lawry's first. The meal was wonderful; I was especially thrilled when served my favorite side dish, traditional English Yorkshire pudding. The strong sense of nostalgia in the air that evening even calmed the tumultuous time Sam and I were experiencing. We would break up one month later.

Gina and I kept in touch, something I encouraged by leaving a generous tip, and she connected me to Mrs. Feathers. When Feathers called me, she said she recalled my sister running around at a Christmas party, and that my father was a dark, Italian-looking man. Feathers remembered! In a very kindly British cadence, she said, "Let me get back to you in a couple of days. I am just going to go through my box of pictures and records."

"That sounds good. Thank you, Mrs. Feathers." I hung up and within the hour received a call about a job that I had been pursuing for over six months. *They finally hired me! First Feathers, and now this job! Fantastic*, I thought. I wish I had known just how fantastic my Feathers connection would be then. Sometimes when a door opens, it opens so wide the hinges nearly fall off.

A few days later, I received another call from Mrs. Feathers. "Your mom worked with a woman named Marcy, who is still in touch with all of the Lawry's people." Feathers said she would e-mail me within the week. I was floored. Never had I ever had to rely so completely on the kindness and effort of perfect strangers before, but it was finally panning out for me.

The very next day, I received an e-mail from Marcy, in

which she described how she had worked with my mom, and how they had been very close because they were both Jewish women around the same age. She recalled a time where my mother and a coworker, Anne Marie, were held up at gunpoint at the restaurant. "I have not spoken to Anne Marie in over twenty years, Jessica, but she would be a great person for you to speak with." Finding Anne Marie seemed impossible, though, as Marcy was sure she had married and then most likely moved out of the Los Angeles area.

Marcy, like most of the other servers, was an aspiring actress. All they cared about were the tips and forming good relationships with coworkers so that they could call last-minute to have someone cover their shift if they were so lucky as to get an audition, Marcy told me. That never would have occurred to me. "Dianne was a great waitress on her own merit. She was not trying to entertain, like we all were. Your mother sincerely cared about the company, the restaurant, and the happiness of the customers," Marcy said. "Boy, could her smile light up a room."

Several months later, I met Marcy in person. She had striking red hair, and I could tell she was someone my mother would have been drawn to. I immediately felt at ease with her on that warm spring morning. She brought me a picture of the Westside Broiler staff in costume during the Halloween when my mother was sick, in 1983. Everyone looked so goofy and happy. Marcy then connected me with Bryan, my mother's manager and good friend.

I remembered having met Bryan as a child. All of my mom's doctors were in Los Angeles, so during hospital breaks she would drop by the restaurant and say hi to him. I can remember

her telling my dad to give her privacy so she could talk with
Bryan alone, like in the old days. It's interesting that my mom
and I have both had so many cherished male friends yet so
much trouble dating. One would think being friends with men
would make you better at reading them, but that is apparently
not accurate. In Bryan's own words, "Your mom was not one to
drop a friendship."

Knowing the closeness they'd shared, I did not hesitate to
call Bryan at his office that spring.

"This is Bryan," he answered.

"Hi, Bryan. You may not remember me, but I am Dianne
Barraco's daughter Jessica."

A long silence followed. "Of course I remember you! Wow,
Dianne. I miss her," he replied in one full breath.

"I know. You two were close."

He responded, "I can see her laughing and smiling at me
from the kitchen right now. The vision I have of her is so
vivid," he said. I was not expecting him to disclose such powerful emotion so early in our conversation. Perhaps my mom
really did have her ways with men, or perhaps the fact that she
was such an aggressive person made it easier for her to find
friendship with men.

After a few months of correspondence, Bryan offered to
meet me at Lawry's for dinner. That evening, Bryan told me
that it did not surprise him that there was someone else in my
mother's life. While he knew she loved Ray, it was not as much
as he loved her. "Dianne would have run him over with a car if
he got in her way," Bryan said to me over our three-hour meal
together. Of course, I was hoping he would know about my
mother's relationship with Frank.

Sitting there with him, I again felt my mother's presence. The gong sounded. "What's that for?" I asked Bryan.

"That means there's a fresh pot of coffee made. We've been doing that since your mom worked here."

The Westside Broiler struggled for most of its history, paralleling my mother's own long-standing inner turmoil. "Your mom was the ruler of the roost, even though she never had a title above waitress," Bryan said. She must have felt a deeper connection with the Broiler and wanted to make sure it succeeded to the very best of her abilities. "No one messed with her; she was too formidable."

I smiled, knowing my sister and I share that strength with her. The "Dianne bitch-out" was not just a phrase our family knew; everyone knew not to piss her off unless they wanted a mouthful. And she was usually in the right.

"She was a tough cookie," Bryan said. "Dianne would lean up against the back room, with her hands folded, kind of taking in the scenery and observing the nightly atmosphere. When she got sick, I told her not to come in. I thought she should take more time off, but even when she lost her hair, she came to work wearing a wig," he continued.

"She still looked good with the short hair," I admitted.

I could remember going to wig shops with my mom growing up. I had thought it was normal for women in their early forties to need several wigs. I used to go into her walk-in closet, play with her jewelry box, and play with the wigs on the Styrofoam mannequin heads. A tear rose in the corner of my right eye as I thought about how I hadn't understood the severity of her health—I had thought she was lucky to be playing dress-up.

Bryan smiled, and I swallowed my sadness with one gulp of water. "Yes. She was so beautiful. She loved strong men, too."

The importance of commanding self-respect was something my mother taught me at a young age. "Nobody is going to give you respect the way you can." This went along with "to each his own" and "kill 'em with kindness." Although common expressions, the ones my mom chose had been validated by her unique life experience. Among many other life lessons, she taught me to accept people for their differences, and also to beat them at their own games. It still stuns me, but people seem always to be playing games, especially at the office and, oddly, in love.

Bryan interrupted my thoughts: "She let me know she had something else going on [romantically] more or less, without saying anything directly." Bryan recalled another waitress my mother was close friends with, Anne Marie. I figured if Anne Marie were important, she would present herself to me. And she did.

A few months after I had dinner with Bryan, Marcy gave me a call. "I have some interesting news," she said. "I found Anne Marie, or, rather, she found me." I was astonished. I thought no one had heard from her in over twenty years. "Perfect timing for you, huh?" Marcy said. I could hear her wide grin through the phone. "She wants to talk to you. Anne Marie lives in Sacramento now."

"That's great!" I thanked Marcy and got off the phone. I had to think of some questions to ask Anne Marie. I was mostly curious about when she and my mom were held up at gunpoint at the Broiler. This was a "famous" story in my household, and I was excited that I would finally get to talk to another eyewit-

ness about the action scene that had been implanted in my
memory.

THE NEXT DAY, I called Anne Marie. "Hi, this is Jessica
Barraco, Dianne's daughter. Marcy gave me your phone
number."

"Hi, sweetheart!" Anne Marie had the greatest accent, a
beautiful fusion of New Yorker and Grecian goddess. Her voice
revealed her physical beauty. Harvey had spoken of her delicate
figure and silky black hair. Her beauty was comparable to my
mother's. Some of their coworkers speculated this was why
they were such good friends: they knew what it was like to be
envied.

"We used to count tip money together and have a drink at
the end of the night," Anne Marie recalled. On the night of the
hold-up, my mom had parked her car in front of the restaurant.
Anne Marie had hers in the back, so she offered to drive my
mom to the front. They assumed that would be the safest way
to get to their respective cars.

"Thanks for the offer, Anne," my mom had said, stepping
outside.

The next thing they knew, a medium-size man wearing a
stocking mask and gloves pointed a gun at Anne Marie's
stomach. "Where's the money?" he shouted. Dianne kept her
cool as he demanded they go to the rear of the restaurant. The
assistant manager was already in the back, putting the money in
the drop slot. "Get on the floor and give me the money," the

gunman demanded. When he got what he wanted, he ripped the phone off the wall, slammed the door, and fled. The three of them were under the office table for about ten minutes.

"It felt like hours," Anne Marie told me, recalling it all. "Then we all went to have a drink," she laughed softly.

"Dianne had a lot of male friends." Anne Marie relayed the same thing I had heard many times. "It wasn't that she didn't like women; she just related better to men somehow." Anne Marie went on to tell me that they had been the two most-requested waitresses, and about the prestige that went with working at a high-quality Beverly Hills restaurant during those days.

"Your mom was a fabulous waitress," she said. "We used to make tableside Caesar salads and carved the meat with smiles on our faces."

Anne Marie went on to talk about the movie stars they waited on, and of course mentioned Rock Hudson. "We were proud to be waitresses." The conversation ended on a note similar to my talk with Bryan. "I am proud to say I knew her," she concluded. "Dianne touched my life."

*D*ianne had tried to stop seeing Frank. But being with him was powerfully addictive, and she did not believe that any form of therapy could help her.

Mirroring that vexation was a cold that would not go away. Dianne had been feeling weak. The stress of being a young mother, hardworking waitress, and wife, and her nightlife, all seemed to be catching up with her. In the second month of her chest congestion, she finally went to the doctor. After running a few tests, her general practitioner seemed concerned. He could not find any fluid in her lungs after an initial examination and thought she should get a chest X-ray. Having never had medical problems, Dianne was not concerned. She had the X-ray taken and went about her busy life, working hard and trying to quit her addiction to Frank. She had a love affair with cigarettes as well.

The doctor did not tell Dianne exactly what the X-ray revealed but sent her immediately to an oncologist. Ray was working that day, so she asked her mom to accompany her. She continued to believe nothing was seriously wrong.

"Dianne Barraco," Dr. Ben Schwartz said, briskly walking into the sanitized room in a crisp white lab coat.

"Yes, Doctor. That's me."

"It's very nice to meet you," he went on. "I am so sorry to tell you this, but you have a tumor the size of a grapefruit on your chest. It has to be removed immediately, and you must start chemotherapy directly after the surgery."

Stunned by what the doctor had said, Dianne just stared into space, but Ethel broke into tears and grabbed her hand.

Dianne felt numb. Tears welled up in her throat, but she pushed them back down, swallowing hard. "I have a three-year-old daughter, Ben." She added politely, "Can I call you that?"

He smiled. "Yes, you may."

"I cannot die. I won't die. I will fight this grapefruit thing on my chest."

Ben, a bright, young oncologist, told her that Dianne was the kind of patient everyone spoke of in medical school. She was the type who just might be able to beat the most aggressive form of cancer, out of sheer will and determination, and survive.

"How soon can I have the surgery?" Dianne asked blankly.

Ray used every penny he had for Dianne's surgery. Her tips could pay rent that month. Ray's mother flew in from the East coast, bringing toys and clothes to distract her granddaughter from her mother's absence. The sickness was so terrifying that Ray and Dianne had really come together.

The surgery went well. It was quite invasive, and they had to make an extremely long incision vertically down Dianne's chest, but it was successful. Dianne would have the scar for the rest of her life. It would remind her of how strong she was, though it was hideous-looking.

While Dianne was still in the hospital, Ray stayed home from work for a couple of days. One day, the phone rang. Ray was home alone. "Hello," Ray answered.

"Hi there. I was just calling to see if Dianne is okay," a man's deep voice said.

Ray asked who was on the line, although he already knew.

"I'm Frank. I, uh, I have known Dianne for a long time. I'm just concerned, Ray." Frank sounded like he had been crying.

Ray hung up the phone furiously. Ray, by this point, knew all about Frank and Dianne's past and present.

When Dianne came home from the hospital the next day, she discovered two-dozen beautiful red roses waiting for her. At first, she tensed up. She was scared they had come from Frank. Then Ethel came running into the room, wearing her favorite powder-blue dress, saying hello in her high-pitched voice. "It's nice to see you, too, Mommy." Dianne smiled, though she felt very weak. Using dry shampoo for ten days straight had not done much for her vanity, either.

"Do you know who these flowers are from?" her mother asked her.

Dianne shook her head no, praying the answer would not be Frank. Her heart skipped a quick beat.

"*Rock Hudson!*" Ethel squealed like a little girl.

"Oh, that is so sweet of him," Dianne said, happy but unfazed. She and Rock had a close rapport that she had never shared with her family, but Dianne just wanted to live at this point. She was preoccupied. She was worried about her marriage, her love for Frank, and for her daughter's future if she kept this lie up. Things could not keep going on like this. So Dianne made a choice and never looked back.

Ring, ring. Ring, ring. Dianne dialed the number she knew by heart. He picked up.

"It's me. Please don't say anything. We can stay friends—I hope we do—but we have to stop this. I am a sick woman."

Frank sighed on the other end of the line and said, "We'll always have the ballroom, baby."

Tears started to well up in Dianne's eyes as she hung up the phone. For the first time ever in their history together, she had bade him goodbye.

Ray walked into the room shortly after that with the chicken soup and ginger ale she had requested. "Thank you, honey," Dianne said. "You really are the best husband, and I want you to know that from now on, I will be the best wife in return."

On the radio, the song "You Are the Sunshine of My Life" came on. Unlike any man she had ever been with before, Ray accepted Dianne's apology; he accepted her flaws.

She suddenly noticed her surgical wound start to itch a little, which was a good thing. Her scar was healing, the tumor was gone, at least for now, and so was the burden. If only surgery could remove the cavernous longing in her heart. For Frank? For life? She suddenly wasn't sure. Dianne closed her eyes for a moment and then got up. It was time for more chemotherapy.

*I*t was well past 3:00 a.m. as I walked alone up Third Avenue to my apartment. Two seconds before, I had been walking arm in arm with someone I really liked. Someone older, who had just told me that I had a lot to learn. The ironic thing was that I could probably have taught him a thing or two. I suddenly wished I were on my old block in Chelsea—the one where my mom lived, or at least our names did. It was etched in the cement: "Jessica [hearts] Dianne." Whenever I was upset walking home, I would see this and smile, no matter what. But on the East Side, my usual fearful thoughts of walking alone at night escaped me. I didn't care just then. All the thief would get out of me was a good scream, a useless debit card with a small balance on it, a Sexy Mother Pucker lip gloss, and a few tampons.

Bring it on, I thought. The alcohol was not serving me well. Maybe it never did. I said out loud to nobody, "I don't get it! Frank was at least eight years older than Mom. He didn't care." Someone passed me, likely thinking, *Who is this crazy girl with the pretty shoes?* I didn't care at that moment. At that moment, I felt full of rage. I felt confused. I felt raw. I felt like I wished surgery could have removed the part of me that longed to be loved. The part of me that missed out on so much uncon-ditional love that I craved it like a drug addict needed his morning shoot-up.

I was angry at her for the first time maybe ever. I was angry at her, I was angry at Frank, I was angry at that person who bade me goodbye at Twenty-Third Street, three blocks too early and six months too late. He shouted at me, "Get that book pub-lished, Jessica! I want a signed copy—on my mantel. Don't be a stranger." I said nothing, for the first time ever. I had no words. In my opinion, that person had chosen to be a stranger in my life. He was scared of the passion that might have existed between us. He appeared to be sincere, like so many. But what made sincerity sincere, anyway? What was the discrepancy that made sincerity actually genuine? Was there something I was missing, or was it simply always a possibility to bid someone goodbye without saying it—turning a tearful eye to look away from a person who could be somebody? A person who might have held you one night when you were cold, a person who might have been there to witness an exciting phone call about the very book he wanted on his mantel, a person who might one day have been there for a spiritual sign from my mother?

To me, that was the most exciting and frustrating part of life: you never knew who the person would be to you in the future. Even though the night was bleak, I still had no idea what could happen next. Nobody did—not even him, not even his mantel. What I was sure of was that when stubborn people made up their minds about you, that would be how you stagnantly stayed in their hearts.

I woke up hung-over, dehydrated, and with a pounding headache that felt like a tiny monkey was slapping a cymbal in between my temples. Shivering from the raw emotions stirred up the night before, I tried my best to compose myself. After I'd spent three years doing my best to find Frank, researching Columbus Recreation, and looking up phone numbers online and in library-archived telephone books, my search was incomplete yet the best I could do on my own. I couldn't afford a private investigator. Lucky for me, a friend had introduced me to one who was, like me, an alumnus of the University of Colorado, so he cut me a break financially. I had scoured the entire country for Frank Parker. I would give my left arm to find him. I had climbed the Mount Everest of investigative journalism trying to. It had taken me years to acknowledge that I had done all that could be done.

I was sitting in my duplex apartment in downtown Manhattan, on the phone with my private investigator, attempting to find Frank. A former CIA agent and protector of six U.S. presidents, The P.I., as he referred to himself, was a sweet guy underneath it all. A Southern gentleman, he had relocated to California in retirement. I had been introduced to him over e-mail, and he did not wish to meet me in person. Privacy was the best policy. Throughout my investigation and discoveries, it had never crossed my mind that if I did find Frank, he might not want to be found. The P.I., having been adopted, had gone on his own search to find his birth parents as a young adult. He was unsuccessful. One of the most valuable things he learned from that experience and later told me was rooted in a famous CIA mantra that he thought applied to both his adoption search and my quest for Frank. When a government official is imprisoned or accused of something, all officials follow a uniform rule: "Admit nothing. Deny everything." Some people just don't want to be found.

A FEW MONTHS BEFORE I'D moved to New York, I'd had lunch with Gloria. She was still married to Ed. She was still the same woman with bright red hair whom I vividly remembered watching in our home movies. She still had the same jolly laugh that she'd shared with my mother as they sat together, talking about life, helping each other learn its lessons along the way. They had both left home at a young age; their lives had been remarkably similar. Like certainly does attract like.

I could see the misery deep in Gloria's blue eyes when she reflected on her upbringing, and how happy it made her that Dianne's daughter had taken the time to research her mother's life with such love and pride. "It's okay, Gloria," I said. She then opened up to me about her family life as if I were my mother.

"Oh, sweetie, I meant to tell ya ..." I looked at her, urging her to go on. "So, I went over to Radio Shack last week to get a CD player, 'cause ya know I like to listen to music at work." I nodded. "Well, anyways, I don't know if I was out of it or what, but I couldn't quite describe what I wanted. I meant to say 'portable' ... well, I just didn't." I smiled, appreciating her wonderful honesty, albeit at times at her own expense. "So I finally told the man who worked there what I wanted, and guess what company made the CD player?" Her eyes lit up.

"Columbus Recreation," we both said in unison.

"Yup," she said excitedly.

"Wow," I responded. "My mom was just saying hi."

Gloria wiped immediate tears from her eyes, her electric-blue eyeliner smudging. Echoing all I had spoken to who knew my mother, she commented, "I still have such a clear picture of her in my head. She was so much fun, your mom." I nodded and smiled. It was almost as if I had been shepherding old friends of my mom's, like Gloria, leading them to realize that it was all right to continue to miss her. I did, every day. A vibrant, authentic person like my mom left a legacy, a legacy that deserved to be honored. No one could ever tell me that my mom did not touch many people's lives; in fact, she still did.

Frank was someone who touched my mother's life deeply. He was the catalyst that put me on the road to a renewed sense of self through my mother's recovered experiences. Frank taught my mom how to dance, and he also indirectly helped me spread my own wings and find my inner groove. The passion I had felt in searching for him had been overpowering. I had never thought I could care that much about anyone or anything I didn't know personally. Caring about Frank and being thankful that he was a part of our lives was powerful. Frank, you must have been one hell of a dancer.

DIANNE

1987

*D*ianne woke up with horrible pains in her abdo-
men. *I cannot believe I am nine months pregnant with a baby at
thirty-seven,* she thought. She knew that having another child
would increase her chances of getting cancer again, but she
wanted to give her daughter a sister. Dianne could imagine
nothing better than having two daughters destined to be "built-
in," best, lifelong friends. *They will have the relationship my sister
and I were supposed to have,* Dianne thought, as sweat dripped
from her forehead.

Against all odds, Dianne had beaten the aggressive lymphoma
five years ago. She was fighting for everything these days. Dr.
Schwartz and her gynecologist had not believed she would ever
be able to get pregnant after all the physical trauma of her debili-
tating chemotherapy and experimental drug regimens, which
administered enough legal poison to destroy the immune system
of an entire population, much less one individual. Neither of
these doctors, both at the top of their game, believed Dianne
would be able to have another child if she survived. But Dianne

had put her mind to it. When a pregnancy test came back positive, her doctors warned her about the risks of carrying the baby to term, but she did not care. She was having this child, and she hoped it would be a baby girl.

"Ray, I think it's time." Ray opened his eyes, looking around the hotel room in Los Angeles, confused. They had recently moved, and Dianne didn't trust doctors in Orange County. It was Monday, August 24.

The day before, the family had been relaxing by the pool at the hotel, videotaping Dianne in a long, blue-striped linen dress. It was an excruciatingly hot summer day. Many mothers-to-be would have scheduled conception to avoid being pregnant in the full heat of August, but Dianne did not have that luxury. Dianne waved at the camera, touching her big belly, thanking God she had been able to carry the baby to term, with few, if any, repercussions. She wondered, though, if she might have been pushing her luck to have another child.

"I'll call Dr. Goldberg," Ray said, putting on his jeans and button-down shirt. Dianne took a deep breath as she tried to get out of bed, but plopped back down in sudden pain. She felt like an obese whale. She was ready to get the kid out of her.

Dianne nodded, again trying to get up so she could put her sweatpants on. Once again, she failed. "Jesus fucking Christ, Ray! We have to go," Dianne shouted.

"All right, honey—relax."

"I can't relax!" she screamed, in acute pain. Dianne went to get a glass of water from the table in the middle of the room and nearly fell. "Get me water," she demanded, as sweat dripped from every pore.

Dianne couldn't believe the pain she was in. She was two

weeks overdue, and the sweltering heat hadn't helped either. *Never again will I have a pregnancy that ends in the summer,* she told herself. She had survived cancer, dealt with few complications during the pregnancy, and worried every day about her doctors' warning that she might not be healthy enough to bring her baby to term and that the baby's health could be in jeopardy. Her body was so beaten up; what if the doctors were right? How could she be so sick, put her body through so much trauma, and expect to give birth to a healthy newborn? Dianne scolded herself and wondered if this was another one of her mistakes. Maybe her first-born would be the only thing she got right in this world.

Dianne knew she was an incredibly bitchy pregnant woman. In times like these, a girl really needed her best girlfriend around, supporting her if she bitched out a nurse, told a doctor to move faster, or commanded her husband to "shut the hell up." Dianne always believed that men too often made things worse, rather than better.

They went off in the silver Volvo station wagon they had bought for their growing family. Dianne had wanted a black car with a tan interior but did not get that until a few years later. For now, they had the station wagon, which represented everything Dianne's childhood had not: safety, security, and unconditional shelter.

Dianne just cried. "Get me out of this car and into the hospital!"

She said the Sh'ma, a Jewish prayer that one recites to give thanks, which Dianne always said to ward off potential danger. Years of being a reckless teenager had led her to praying a whole hell of a lot, and she repeated this prayer every time a plane she was on landed or took off, to ensure her safety. She kept repeating the Sh'ma over and over until they turned into the parking lot at Cedars-Sinai hospital, the same hospital she had been born in.

The nurses came to help her out of the car and into a wheelchair. "Goldberg! Dr. Goldberg! Where the fuck is he?" Dianne screamed.

"He's on the third floor and will be with you shortly," a blond nurse said excitedly.

Of course, Dianne thought. *I have to have the blond, peppy nurse who is more excited about this baby than I am, even though I've risked my life for it.* She gave Ray a classic Dianne expression that said, *Change the fucking nurse, now.*

Ray pulled the nurse aside and requested the nurse Dianne had had with their first child. Even though that had been nine years before, it was worth a shot.

"You know," the nurse replied, "Nina's actually working today."

"Great," replied Ray. He turned back to Dianne. "Let me get you comfortable in your delivery room, and then I will go get her." Dianne gave a thumbs-up sign, trying to do her Lamaze breaths.

Once in her delivery room, Dianne sat upright in the bed, watching the door for the anesthesiologist and Dr. Goldberg with a scowl on her face. In excruciating pain, she drifted off into a reverie about the life of a butterfly.

A butterfly's life cycle fascinated Dianne. When it broke out of its chrysalis, its wings were at first wet and crumpled. *They are screwed from the beginning*, she thought. The butterfly then exerted great effort by pumping blood into its new wings. Somehow, they expanded. This was nearly instantaneous. Once its wings were dry, the butterfly was ready to fly away and search for its food. Not all butterflies hatched out of their chrysalis right away; some spent the winter months inside and hatched in the summertime, just like Dianne's second baby would. One sad truth about butterflies was their life span. On average, a butterfly survived for only one month, so it found a mate quickly to guarantee the existence of butterflies in nature for generations to come. The other sad thing was that a butterfly never knew its parents. One butterfly would rarely live to see its child break through the chrysalis and fly.

Dianne could relate to these beautiful metaphors. She had thought her mate was Bill Mercer, but fate had cut his life short. And then she had thought it might be Wayne, and then Frank, and now Ray. Dianne very much hoped they would stay happy together, because she knew that life was hard to endure alone. Between contractions, Dianne breathed and smiled, remembering the times she had shared with each of these men. After all of the drama and all of the triumphs, she could see everything come together. She could see the unique beauty in all of her experiences and relationships, though some had been brief. Dianne was wise enough to know that even short-lived beauty was precious and worth enduring, even if you suffered a great loss in the end.

"Hello, Dianne," Dr. Goldberg announced loudly, lifting her out of her reverie. "How's our girl doing?"

"Hello. I'm fucking uncomfortable," Dianne replied, with a smile. She was one of the few women who can swear while maintaining their feminine charm.

"Let's take a look," Dr. Goldberg said, and smiled. He was used to Dianne's disposition. They had seen a lot of hard times together, but he hoped this delivery would not be one of them.

"Well, you're six centimeters dilated, so it shouldn't be long now," he announced. "Great," Ray said.

Dianne was still stressed. "Get me some ice chips, please," she said to Ray. She smiled sweetly at Dr. Goldberg.

"I will be back in about ten minutes, Dianne. Don't go anywhere, okay?" He smiled and closed the door. Ray went to get the ice chips, and Dianne was temporarily alone. She was terrified. She just kept saying to herself, *I hope this baby is all right; she deserves a good life. Her life will be better than mine.*

She wanted to reach for the phone and call Donna, to tell her to drive from San Diego to be with her, but she knew her old friend would never make it in time. Even though Donna had seldom visited Dianne since her marriage to Ray, Dianne wanted her there just then, badly. Dianne's marriage at fifteen had changed their friendship, and their lives since then had diverged dramatically. Donna had changed—she had even become the perfect housewife. Who would have thought?

Four o'clock . . . The clock was running. *Tick, tick, tick.*

When Dr. Goldberg came back, everything got better. "Now, push, Dianne! The baby is crowning." It was 4:20 in the afternoon.

"Where's Ray?" Dianne shouted, exasperated. The doctor and nurse exchanged glances. "Find him!"

"One more push, Dianne!"

"Where's Ray?" Dianne screamed. "I need him!"

Just then, Ray rushed into the room, sweating and out of breath. "Did I miss it?" he said.

Ray took Dianne's hand as she endured one last painful contraction and took one last Lamaze breath. Dianne squeezed Ray's hand until all of their knuckles were white and their fingers swollen. Dianne held her breath on and on and on....

"And the baby's out," Dr. Goldberg said, pleased with how little time the delivery had taken, although it had seemed like an eternity to Dianne. "Congratulations, Dianne. You have another girl," he said.

While the nurse suctioned the baby's nose and mouth, Ray looked at Dianne and said, "Another girl. Now you have two girls, just like you wanted."

Dianne's throat choked up with emotion. She had done another thing right: she had given birth to another healthy baby girl. After all she had been through, the stressful upbringing, the lymphoma, the chemotherapy, the heartache, she had what she wanted: a beautiful family and two daughters she could raise to be close—closer than she and her sister had been. They would learn from each other, protect each other, and never be alone.

The nurse handed Dianne her new daughter, Jessica. For the first time, my small brown eyes met my mother's green ones, and they said, "I love you." Well, Dianne said it out loud, but I'm sure I was thinking it too.

"My Sheynah Meydeleh," Dianne said, meaning "beautiful face" in Yiddish "What beautiful hands you have. And what gorgeous fingers," she said, interlocking her pinky and ring fingers with her newborn's, showing off the baby's squeeze reflex.

"You and I are going to be very good friends," she said, and shed a single tear of happiness for the short-lived beauty that the relationship might witness. She always knew she wouldn't live long enough, on some level.

Dianne thought. *I sure have lived one hell of a life.* "Maybe someone will write a book about me one day," she said to no one in particular.

Maybe, like a butterfly, she was too beautiful to live very long. She was always on borrowed time. She had to pass on everything she knew to that baby as quickly as possible, before she was forced to flutter away.

*I*t's a freezing January day in Manhattan. I have just somehow gotten my bundled-up self into a cab, despite the blizzard outside and the flurries in my head. I have a very important interview and have just moved to the city. I need a job desperately.

My phone rings. It's one of my mom's half sisters—one of Sy's daughters from his second marriage—who recently got back in touch with me after not speaking to me for several years. I answer.

"Hi," I say with more than a spoonful of reluctance in my voice.

"You'll never guess what I found, Jessica. It's just the strangest thing."

I say nothing. It takes a lot to shock me these days.

"I was cleaning out the garage, and I found an unmarked brown box full of pictures of Dianne. She was little, like, between the ages of three and five, I'd say."

My heart stops. My hand with the phone in it starts to

shake, so I switch to my left, hoping to God my non-dominant hand will serve me better. "There are dance recital photos, Halloween ... oh, and this really cute picture of your grandmother."

I interject, "Can I ask you if there's a picture of my mom wearing a blue-and-white party dress, bending over, looking to the side with a bow in her hair?" I recall the day, just a couple of months before this moment, when Kim reenacted the scene of the alleged photo that was "to find me" while we channeled my mother. Was she right?

"Yes! I see it—it's right here. Looks like she's leaning against your grandma, in a big brown chair. Have you seen it before?"

I am stunned. I hear, "Jessica, hello?" after a few seconds of much-needed silence. Frost fills the windows, but I feel a furnace ignite in my soul. "No, I've never seen it. It was just something my mom mentioned to me once," I say, grinning.

THE PICTURE IS REAL, in fact. Kim was right: it did find me. I didn't need to look for it. Maybe some things just find you sometimes; perhaps digging just gets you more lost in the shuffle. Some things in life simply shouldn't be that hard. Love, for one. I glance up at the picture now every day—I got it framed in a pink 1950s-style wooden frame. The way I unconsciously positioned it in my room, my mom is looking over her left shoulder and onto my bed. She is still keeping watch over me—all the way from 1953. It's almost like she was born guarding me.

The P.I. has not helped me very much—it turns out I did all of the groundwork myself, with Regina's help. He could not trace the phone number I found in her phone book, and that was the last viable clue I had.

Back at home, I google phrases I have not searched before: "Frank Parker" and "ballroom dancing." One match comes up. My heart drops for the thousandth time along this journey. I am looking at a Frank Parker who looks slightly familiar to me. He is around the same age that Frank would be. It says he's a real estate agent in Nashville. His bio says that he loves ballroom dancing and that he lived in all the places Frank did along the trajectory that I deduced.

"Oh my god," I say out loud to nobody, slowly. I call up Gigi. She tells me I have to call his cell phone number now. That I shouldn't build up the anticipation. I hang up with her and start dialing.

A man answers, a slightly familiar tone to his voice: "Hello, this is Frank." All people of his generation answer their cell this way—as if the caller doesn't know exactly where the person on the other end of the phone is, so the person who answers has to say his name to reaffirm it's actually him.

"Hi, Frank," I stutter. "I'm actually not calling about a listing, although all of your properties look very nice."

"Oh?"

"It's actually, um, interesting. I hope this doesn't take you too aback, but I noticed that you love ballroom dancing, and, um . . . well, did you know someone named Dianne Barraco, or Dianne Harber, in Los Angeles?"

Silence for a few seconds. "Jessica, did you say your name was? I'm going to pull over."

My heart is racing at this point.

"I just pulled over, dear."

"Thanks. You didn't have to do that; I just—"

Frank cuts me off. "I feel bad; you sound so excited there. I'm not the person you seem to be hoping to find. I didn't know your mom. I mean, maybe I knew a Dianne, but—"

This time, I cut him off. "Something tells me you would know exactly who I'm talking about if you did."

"I'm so sorry to disappoint you," this Frank says into the phone.

I am now the one taken aback. It's incredible how sometimes a perfect stranger can feel the gravity of your words over the phone and say exactly what you need to hear at that moment. "Oh, that's okay," I say, clearly devastated through the wire.

"Did you check Arthur Miller Dance, or Third Street Dance Studio, or . . ." His words start to blur together. This man seems to be well versed in the history of the Los Angeles dance scene for a real estate agent in Nashville. What if this *is* the right Frank?

I immediately think of what the P.I. told me before: "Admit nothing. Deny everything." Even if I did ring up the right Frank Parker, he might think I'm his love child looking for money, or he might have a family that he can't explain this to. He might still be in love with my mother. He might be a person who needs to let go of her, as I do of him. Maybe what they had is too sacred to share, even with me. If he opened up the can of worms, his emotions would explode. He buried his feelings for her somewhere in the part of him that was alive in 1981 and is dead now. He does not wish to resuscitate this person. If he opened up, he might not be able to stop. He might lose control again.

We exchange a few more words. "Thanks for the tips, Fra ..." I go to say his name but cannot finish. My heart is too busy sinking and stealing all my words with it, like a passenger without a life jacket clinging to the *Titanic* as it inevitably goes down. I have no more words for him, for this. We exchange formalities and bid each other goodbye.

"I'm sorry I'm not your Frank. I wish I was," he says to me, meaning it.

"Me too," I reply, meaning it, too. A small tear wells up but does not jump out of my eye socket. I have no more tears left for Frank.

I say goodbye to him, and the case is closed. I came so close. But what if it was him? Perhaps he had to pull over to speak to me because he thought he might get into a car accident due to the shock of hearing from Dianne's daughter after all these years. Perhaps he wasn't even in the car at all; maybe he was at home, watching the football game, and when he put me on hold to "pull over," he really went into his desk drawer and pulled out a picture of my mom and him, smiling after winning a cha-cha contest, trophies in hand.

Sometimes I wake up reliving this conversation. When my mind gets off the roller coaster of ifs, whens, buts, and maybes, I can see him in my mind. I can't help but wonder if this Frank was my Frank, my mom's Frank. I can't help but wonder if he's on the other end of the phone, turning a wallet-size photograph taken of my mother in 1973 through his fingers, smiling, knowing that his identity will always be a secret, just like their love story.

L oss. I learned something I never thought I would through losing. I learned a valuable lesson that every mother should relay to her daughters—trust the mystery of life. Trust that it will take care of you. Trust that you might be looking for something that's not there, and trust that you might have found exactly what you're looking for but you will never get confirmation that it's authentic. I learned not to let people craft the journey for me. Life is as real as you let it be. And people, no matter how far away they are, are never truly lost. Memories can fade, but if the passion is strong enough, the feelings never will, and for all other unforeseeable traumas, that is why we passionately write books of memories. Never to let them fade, even if life should somehow force you to forget. There is always someone out there who knows a piece of your mystery and might be willing to share it.

ACKNOWLEDGMENTS

I'd like to give a warm and deep thank-you to She Writes Press, Kamy Wicoff, and Brooke Warner for finally giving my butterfly wings. Thank you to everyone there who has played an integral role in the development and promotion of this book, especially Cait Levin and Annie Tucker. Thank you to my wonderful publicist Erik Deutsch. You helped me back then, and you are still helping me now! Thank you to my super talented copy editor, Molly McGrath. Thank you to Abbey Chaus, my dear friend and film editor—you turned my story into a living, moving piece of art, and I will always cherish my book trailer. And to early readers—fellow memoirist and poet Diana Raab, celebrated fiction authors Simon Van Booy and Christina Baker Kline, Hartford Books Examiner's John Valeri, and Charlee Fam—your time and words mean everything to me.

I'd like to thank all of the perfect strangers who welcomed me into their very personal memories to experience life in their own coming-of-age. Thank you to Gail Carter for joining me on this wild journey and putting your amazing detective skills to work. Thank you to Brian Murphy for connecting me with Van Mercer, because before I found Van, I wasn't sure if I had a romance to tell. Thank you, Van, for all of the pictures, support, and memories of your brother, Bill. He will never be forgotten, so long as I can help it. Thank you to Sheri Kohos for being my first "Westchester advocate" and to Lesley Kasner for putting it all in motion and bringing me to Audrey in her final days. Thank you to Donna Field for inviting me into your home with open arms and always supporting my mother—even in the wings, even today. You have the most beautiful handwriting. Thank you to all the staff at Lawry's Prime Rib for letting my mother and me into your kitchen and making us feel at home there. Thank you especially to Marcy Goldman and Bryan Monfort. Your descriptions of the Westside Broiler and what it was like to work with my mom day-to-day during her first battle with cancer were truly remarkable. Thank you to Glareh Zanganeh for relentlessly supporting me in this and helping me discover my true title. To Catie Chase for always being my biggest cheerleader! To Jen Tenzer for helping me become a hopeful romantic. To my dear sister, Julie Cramer, for supporting me despite the personal matter of this project—I respect you and thank you for helping me become the person I am today. To my three adorable nephews—Jack, Eli, and Henry—for providing enough light in my life to see my way through dark times: you are my tiny but giant inspirations. To Sherrie Toews, for helping me preserve my memories without the pain. I wouldn't be here without you. To my "freditor," Adam Korn, thank you for taking so much time on my story and me. Because of you, I never felt alone, even when doors were being closed—you always saw an open window. To my dear grandma Ann, for giving me the gift of storytelling. It is because of you, Grandma, that I first fell in love with storytelling, and New York. You had all of us spellbound with your words—I miss you every day and feel you in my smile. To the love of my life, Michael Croudo, who may not have been around for the original writing of this book but who does everything in his power to remember my mom and respect our stories, thank you for loving me unconditionally. You are truly my happy ending to this book and I can't wait to spend forever with you.

Finally, to my mom, Dianne Leslie Barraco, for giving me the courage to fearlessly follow my dreams. When I woke up this morning, you were on my mind.

ABOUT THE AUTHOR

photo credit: Max Dionne

Journalist by heart, marketing professional by day, and writer by moonlight, JESSICA BARRACO is a graduate of the University of Colorado, Boulder's School of Journalism and Mass Communication. She published her first newspaper article at nineteen years old, after which she wrote for *Elite Daily*, 944 magazine, and *The Denver Post*. She also spent three years working at HarperCollins Publishers across all of its imprints, working on both nonfiction and fiction books. A member of the Communications Committee of Girls Write Now, a NYC mentorship nonprofit, Barraco lives in New York City.

For more information, please visit:
www.jessicabarraco.com

Follow Jessica:
Facebook at: www.facebook.com/thebutterflygroove
Twitter / Instagram: @obsessjess

SELECTED TITLES FROM SHE WRITES PRESS

She Writes Press is an independent publishing
company founded to serve women writers everywhere.
Visit us at www.shewritespress.com.

*Don't Call Me Mother: A Daughter's Journey from Abandonment to
Forgiveness* by Linda Joy Myers. $16.95, 978-1-938314-02 -5. Linda Joy
Myers's story of how she transcended the prisons of her childhood
by seeking—and offering—forgiveness for her family's sins.

Splitting the Difference: A Heart-Shaped Memoir by Tré Miller-
Rodríguez. $19.95, 978-1-938314-20-9. When 34-year-old Tré Miller-
Rodríguez's husband dies suddenly from a heart attack, her grief
sends her on an unexpected journey that culminates in a reunion
with the biological daughter she gave up at 18.

Don't Leave Yet: How My Mother's Alzheimer's Opened My Heart by
Constance Hanstedt. $16.95, 978-1-63152-952-8. The chronicle of
Hanstedt's journey toward independence, self-assurance, and
connectedness as she cares for her mother, who is rapidly losing
her own identity to the early stage of Alzheimer's.

A Different Kind of Same: A Memoir by Kelley Clink. $16.95,
978-1-63152-999-3. Several years before Kelley Clink's brother
hanged himself, she attempted suicide by overdose. In the after-
math of his death, she traces the evolution of both their illnesses,
and wonders: If he couldn't make it, what hope is there for her?

The Coconut Latitudes: Secrets, Storms, and Survival in the Caribbean
by Rita Gardner. $16.95, 978-1-63152-901-6. A haunting, lyrical memoir
about a dysfunctional family's experiences in a reality far from the
envisioned Eden—and the terrible cost of keeping secrets.

*Where Have I Been All My Life? A Journey Toward Love and Whole-
ness* by Cheryl Rice. $16.95, 978-1-63152-917-7. Rice's universally
relatable story of how her mother's sudden death launched her on
a journey into the deepest parts of grief—and, ultimately, toward
love and wholeness.